FOR ORGANS, PIANOS & ELECTRONIC KEYBOARDS

E-Z PLAY TODAY

21

Good Ol' Gospel

ISBN 978-1-4950-7538-4

HAL•LEONARD®

7777 W. BLUEMOUND RD. P.O. BOX 13819 MILWAUKEE, WI 53213

E-Z Play® Today Music Notation © 1975 HAL LEONARD LLC
E-Z PLAY and EASY ELECTRONIC KEYBOARD MUSIC are registered trademarks of HAL LEONARD LLC.

Visit Hal Leonard Online at
www.halleonard.com

Because He Lives

Registration 2
Rhythm: Fox Trot or Swing

Words and Music by William J. Gaither
and Gloria Gaither

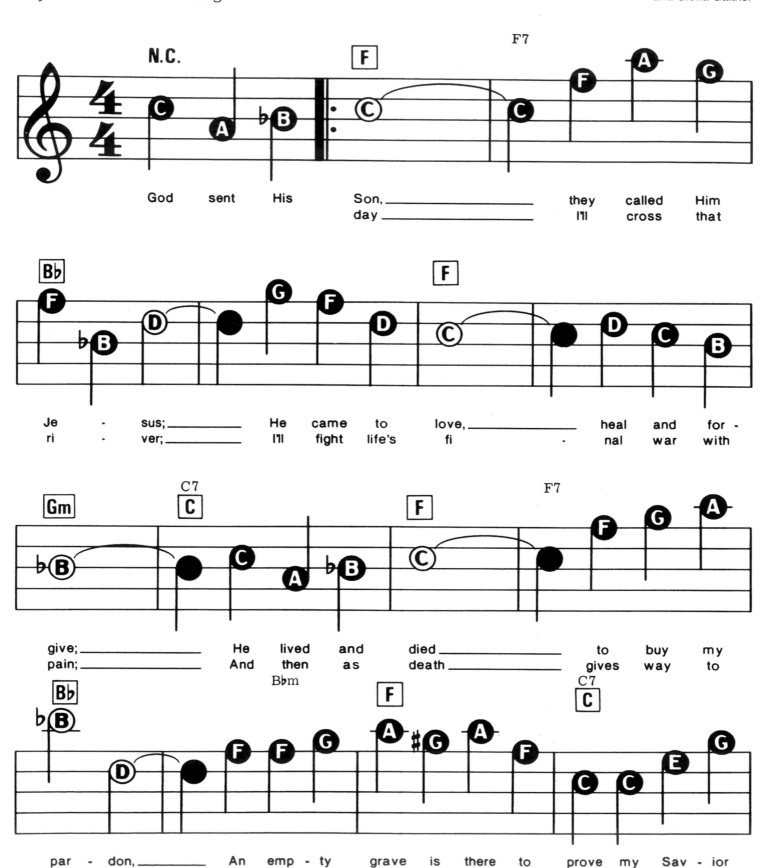

God sent His Son, _____ they called Him
day _____ I'll cross that

Je - sus; _____ He came to love, _____ heal and for -
ri - ver; _____ I'll fight life's fi - nal war with

give; _____ He lived and died _____ to buy my
pain; _____ And then as death _____ gives way to

par - don, _____ An emp - ty grave is there to prove my Sav - ior
vic - t'ry, _____ I'll see the lights of glo - ry and I'll know He

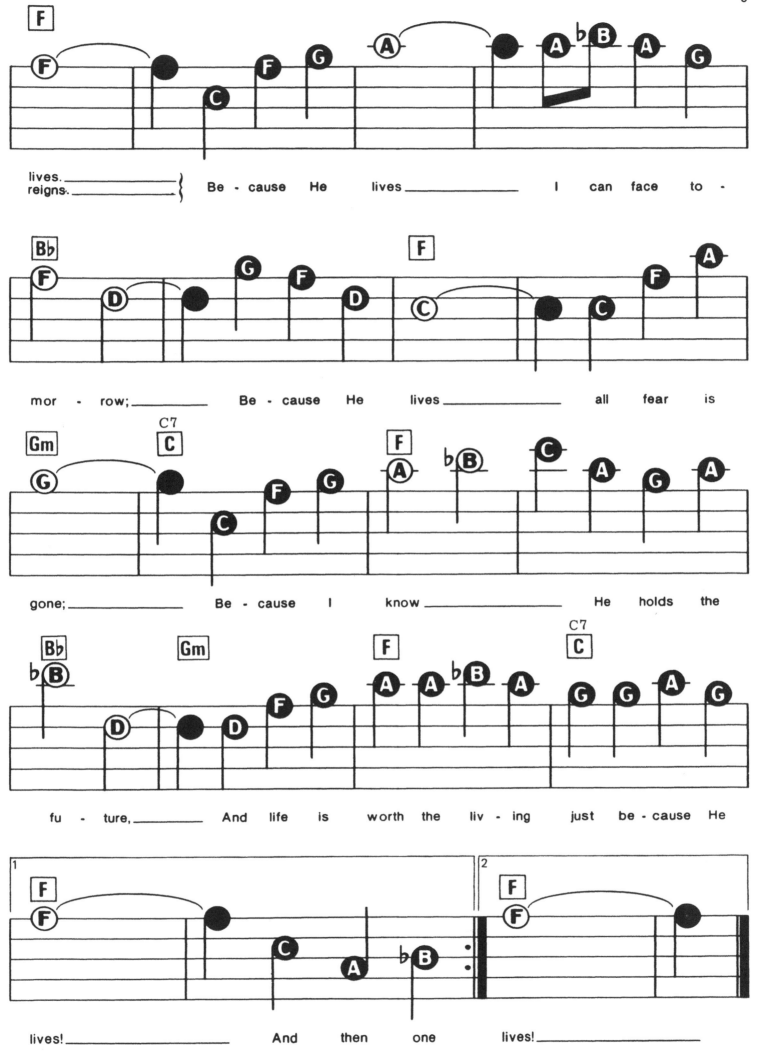

Beyond the Sunset

Registration 4
Rhythm: 8-Beat or Pops

By Virgil P. Brock
and Blanche Kerr Brock

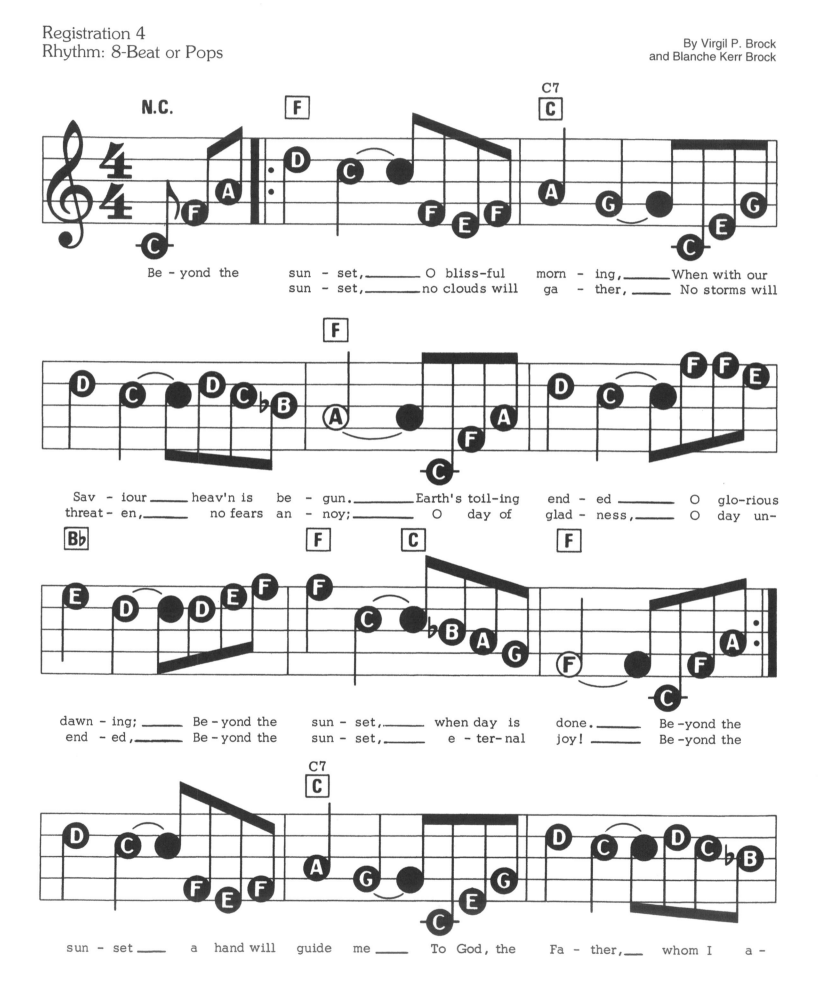

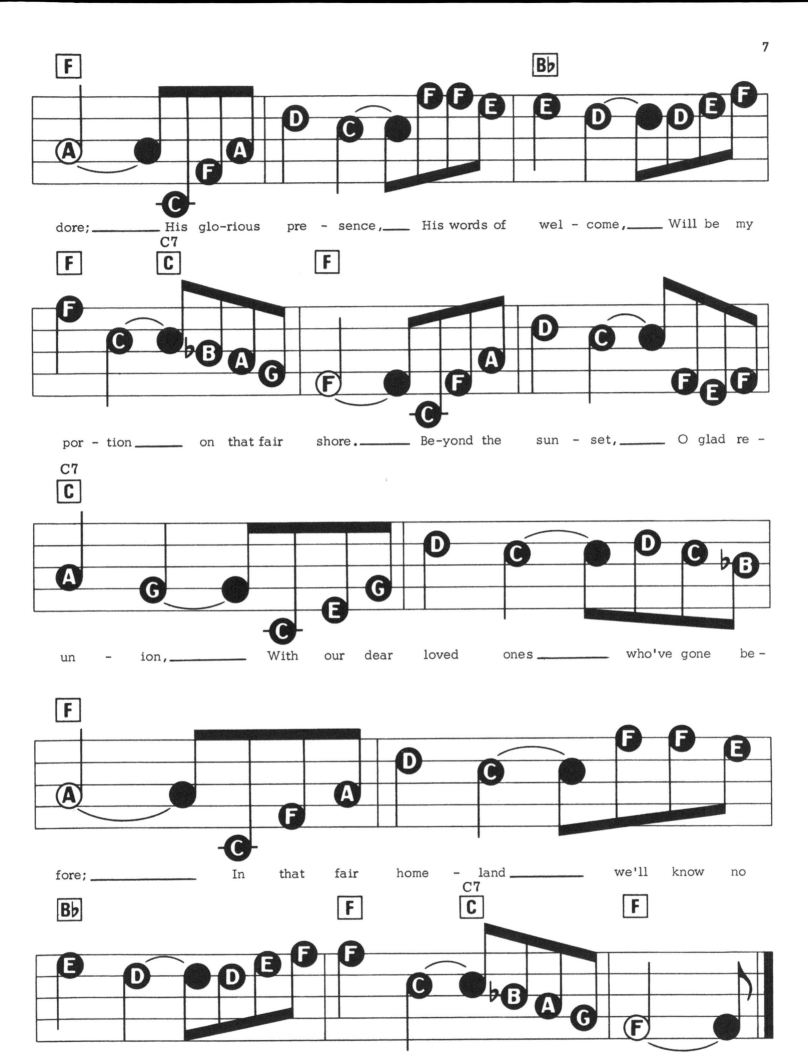

Daddy Sang Bass

Registration 5
Rhythm: Swing

Words and Music by
Carl Perkins

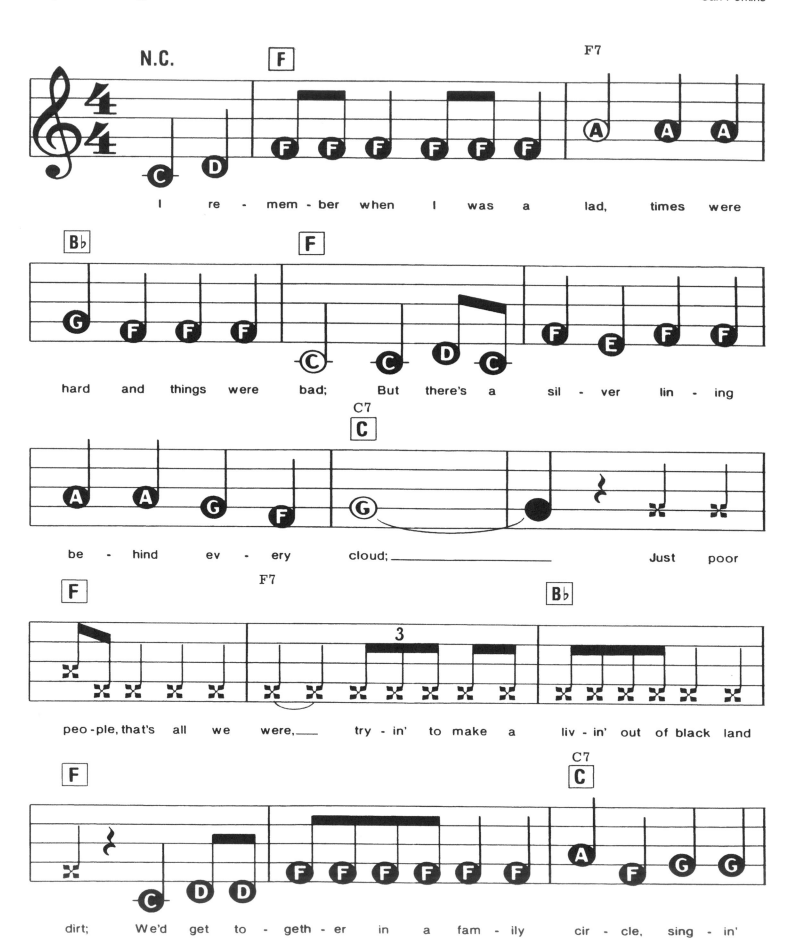

F

loud. _____ Dad - dy sang bass. Ma - ma sang

F7

B♭ F

ten - or, me and lit - tle bro - ther would join right in there,

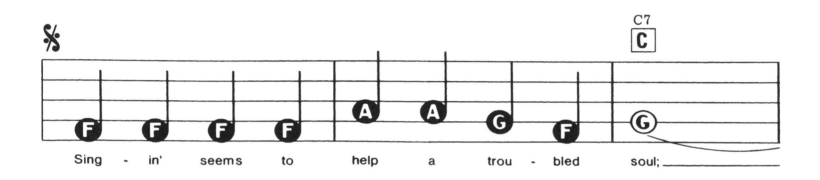

C7
C

Sing - in' seems to help a trou - bled soul; _____

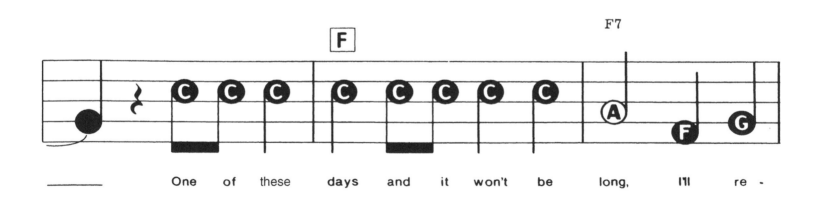

F

F7

_____ One of these days and it won't be long, I'll re -

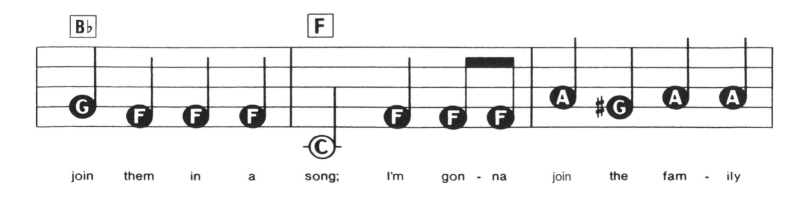

B♭ F

join them in a song; I'm gon - na join the fam - ily

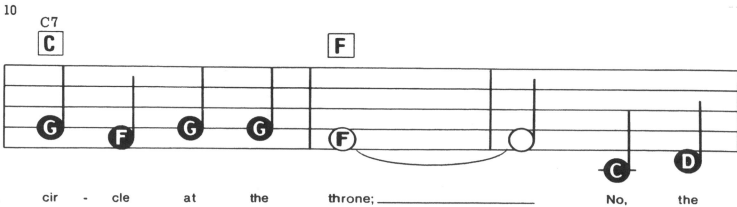

cir - cle at the throne;_____ No, the

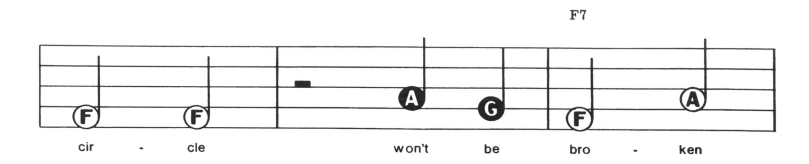

cir - cle won't be bro - ken

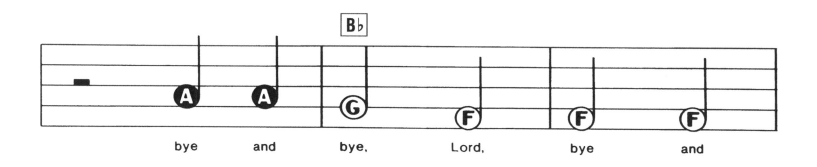

bye and bye, Lord, bye and

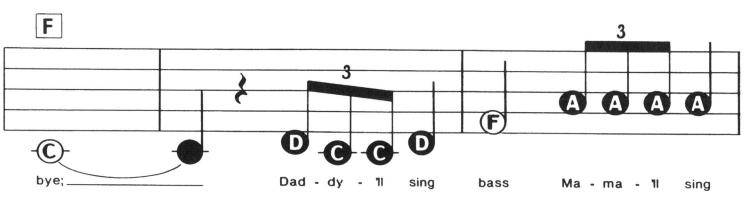

bye;_____ Dad - dy - 'll sing bass Ma - ma - 'll sing

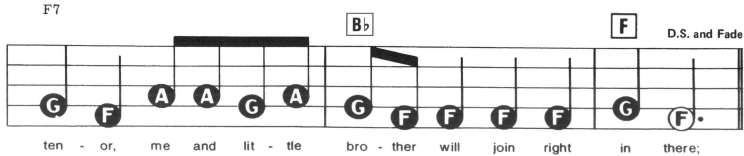

ten - or, me and lit - tle bro - ther will join right in there;

Holy Ground

Registration 3
Rhythm: Ballad or 8-Beat

Words and Music by
Geron Davis

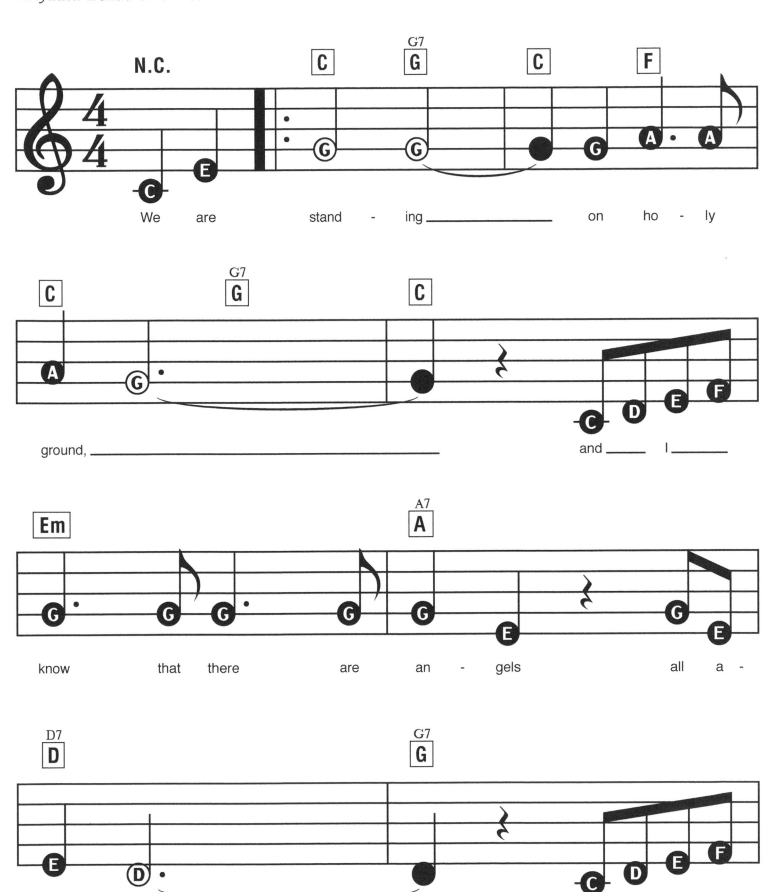

12

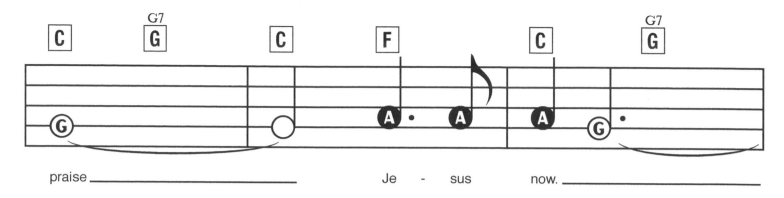

praise _____ Je - sus now. _____

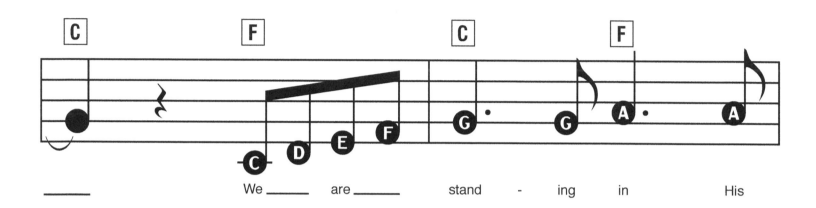

_____ We _____ are _____ stand - ing in His

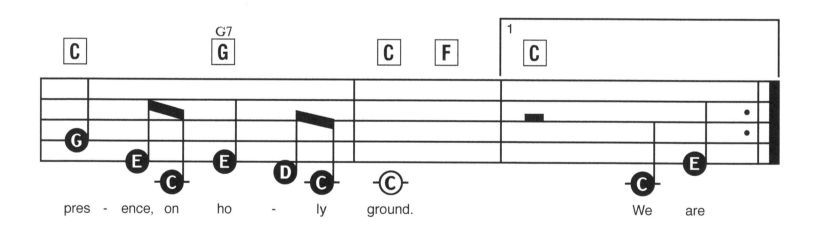

pres - ence, on ho - ly ground. We are

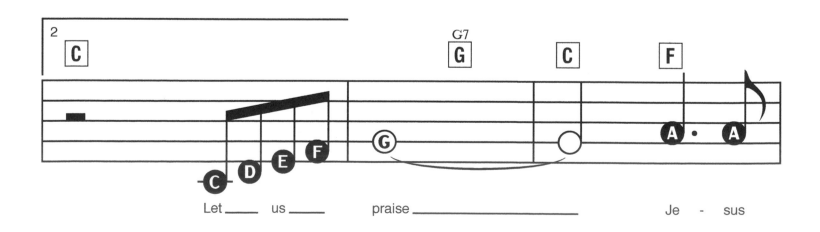

Let _____ us _____ praise _____ Je - sus

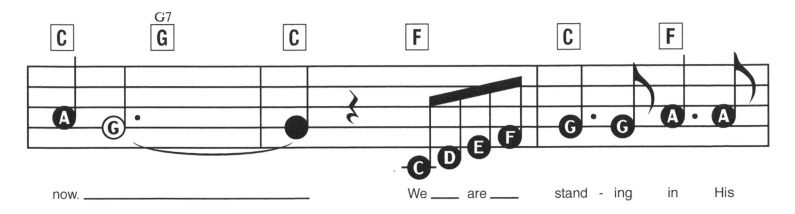

now. _____ We ___ are ___ stand - ing in His

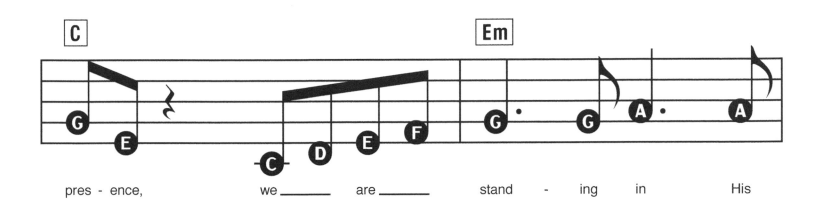

pres - ence, we _____ are _____ stand - ing in His

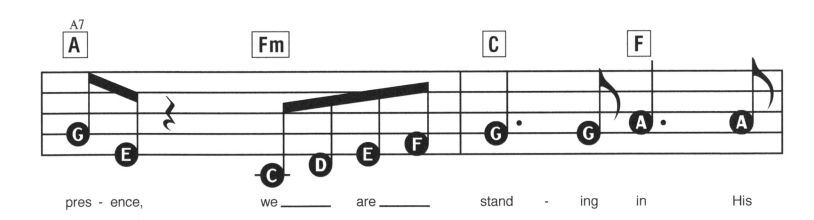

pres - ence, we _____ are _____ stand - ing in His

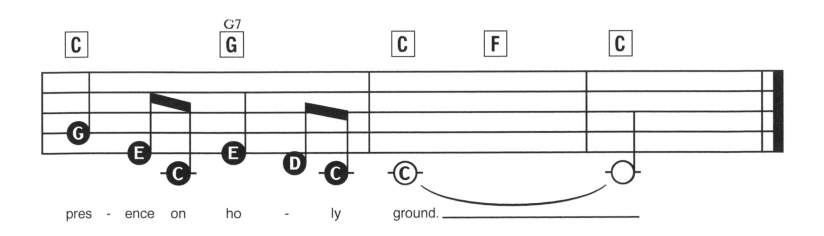

pres - ence on ho - ly ground. _____

Fully Alive

Registration 5
Rhythm: Jazz Rock or Rock

Words by Gloria Gaither
Music by William J. Gaither

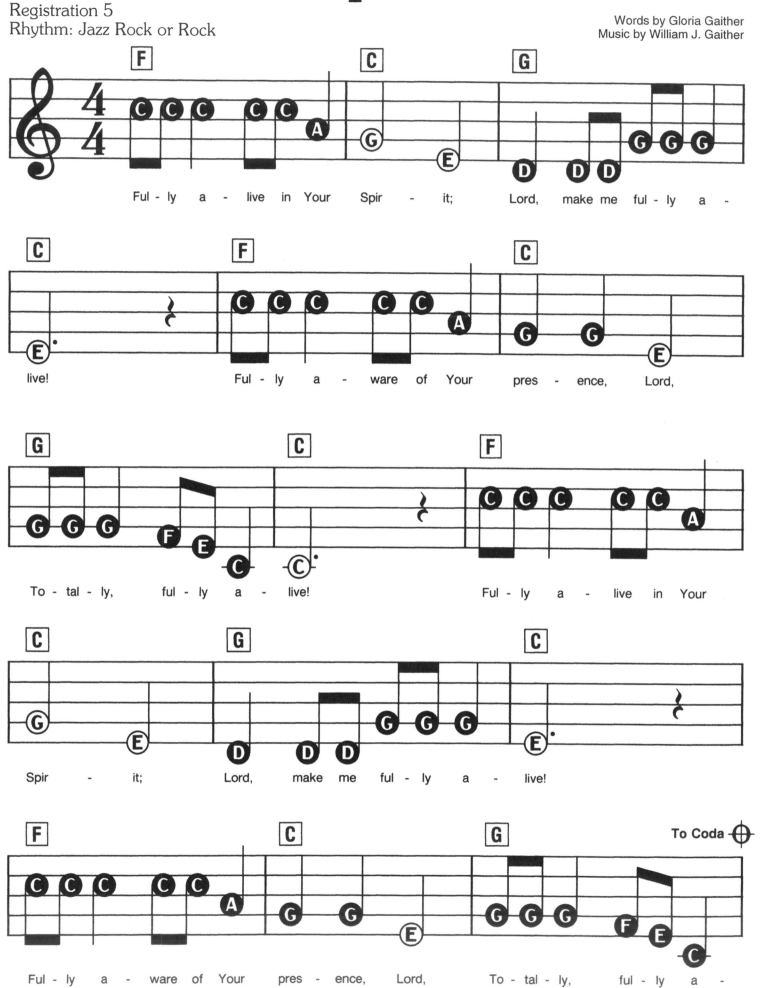

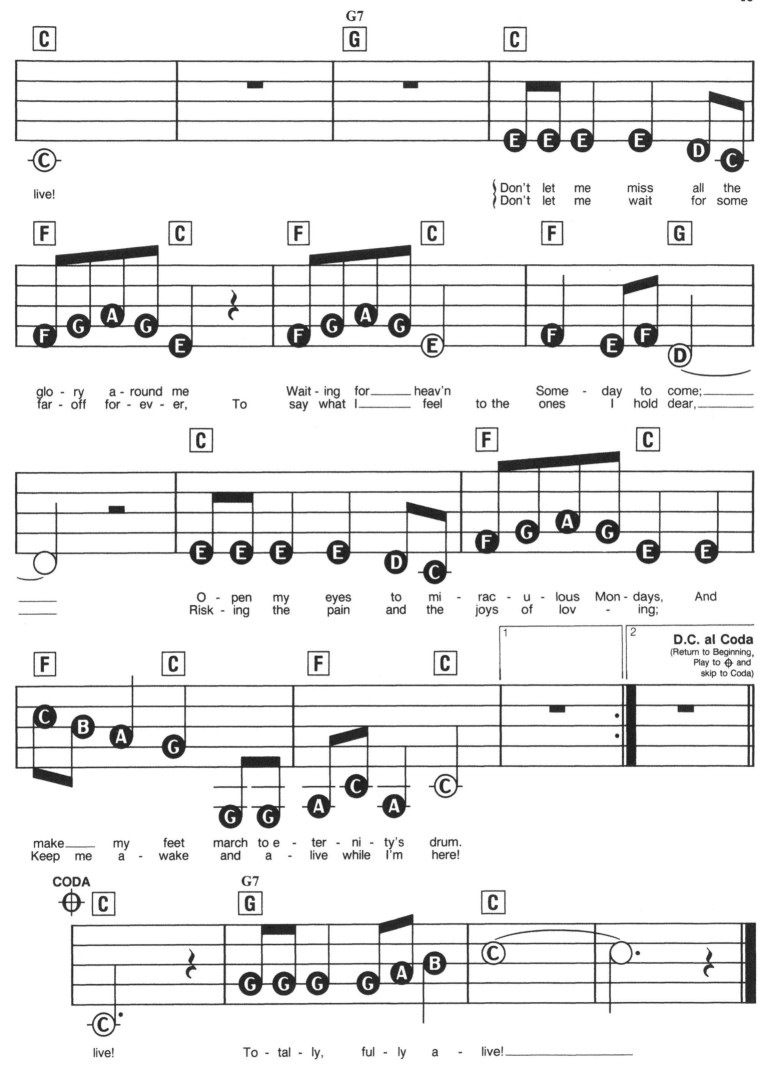

He Touched Me

Registration 2
Rhythm: Waltz

Words and Music by
William J. Gaither

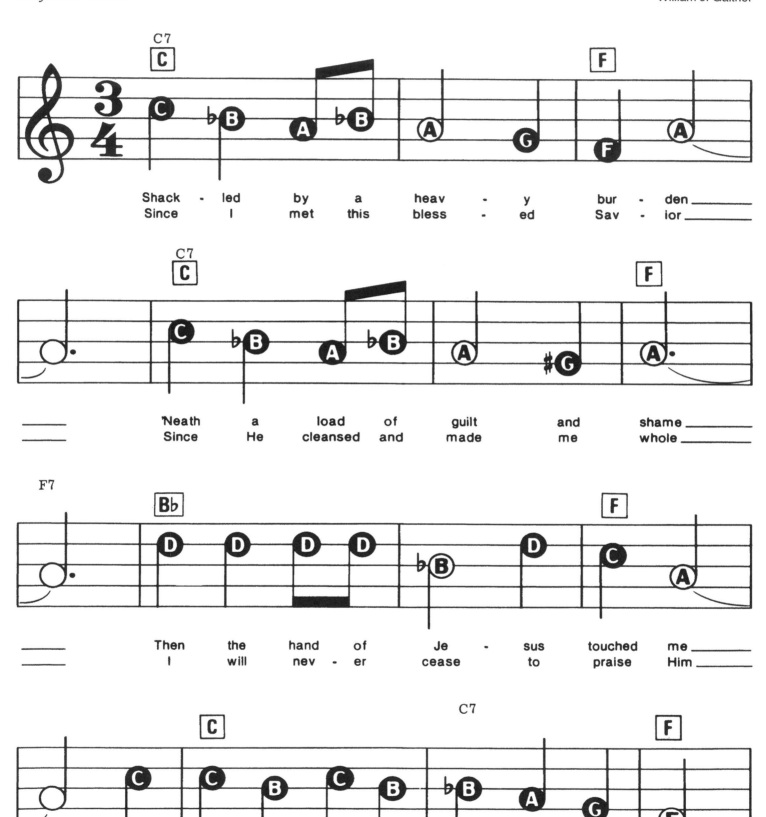

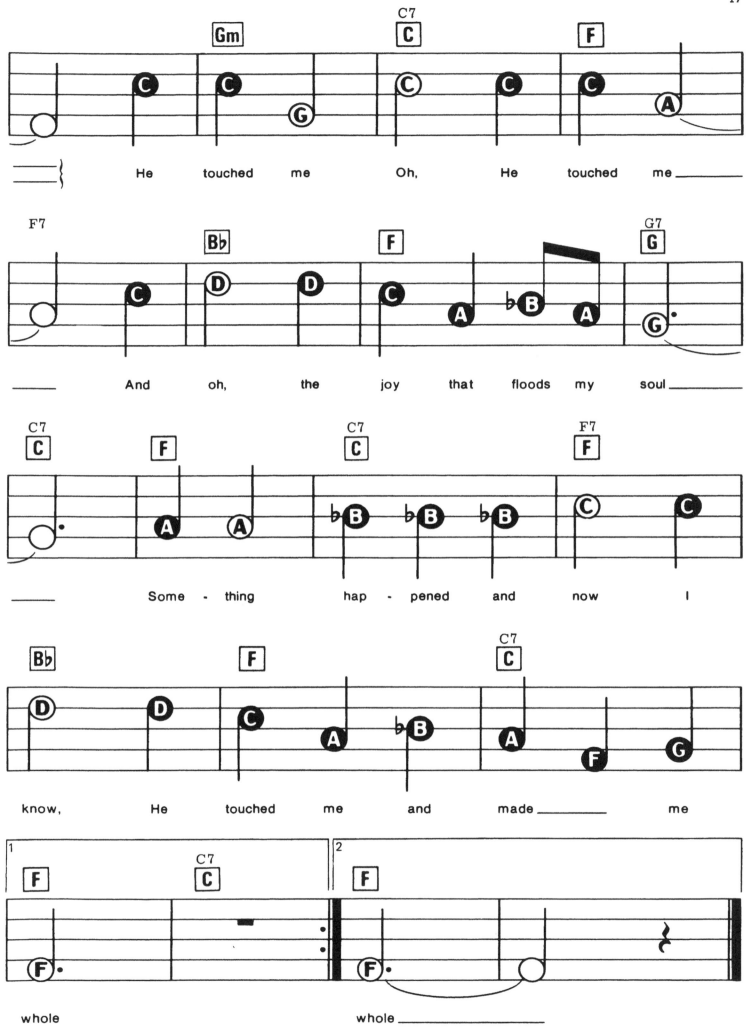

I Believe

Registration 2
Rhythm: Ballad or Slow Rock

Words and Music by Ervin Drake,
Irvin Graham, Jimmy Shirl and Al Stillman

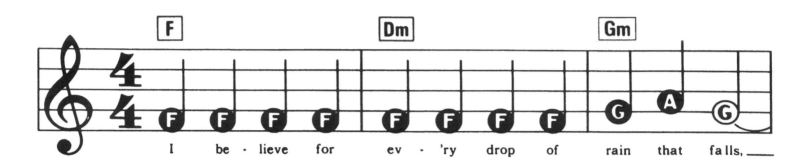

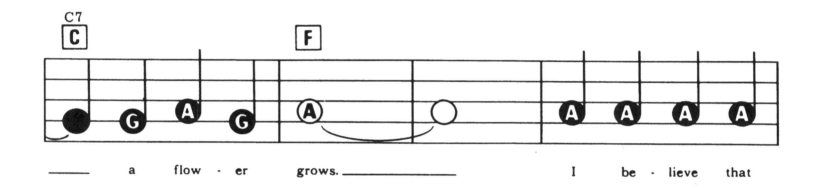

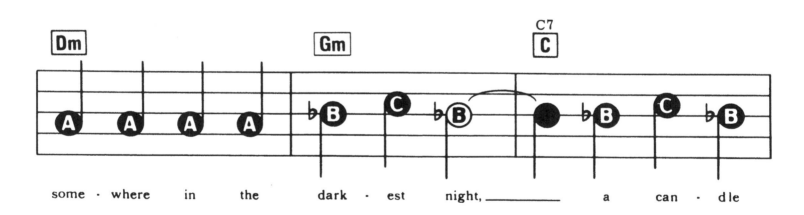

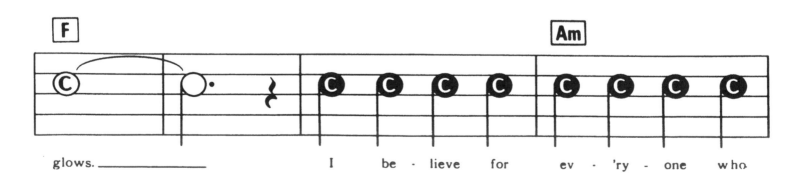

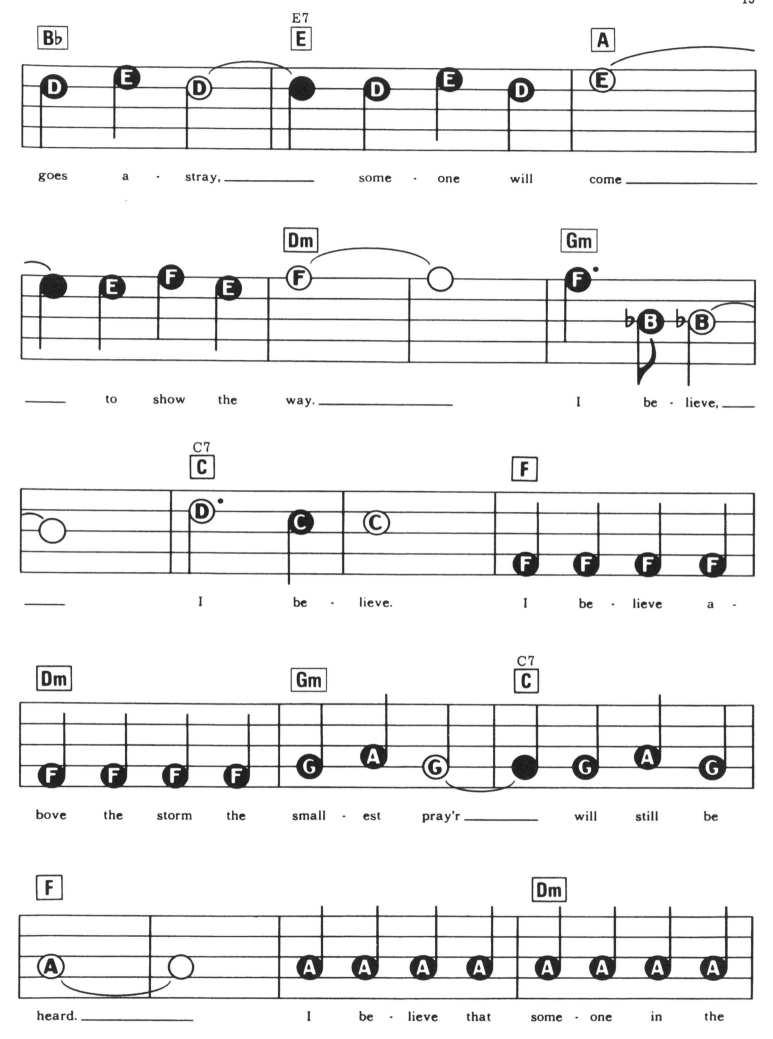

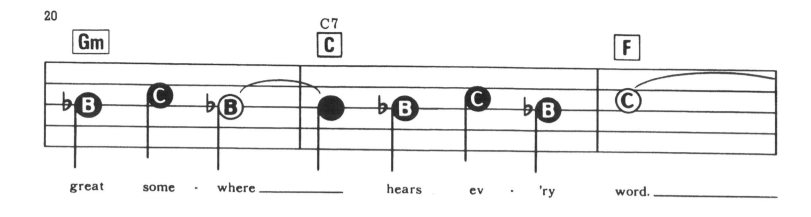

great some - where _____ hears ev · 'ry word. _____

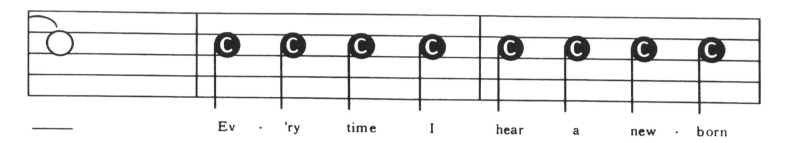

_____ Ev · 'ry time I hear a new · born

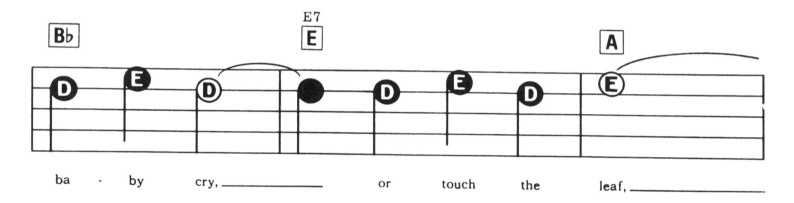

ba - by cry, _____ or touch the leaf, _____

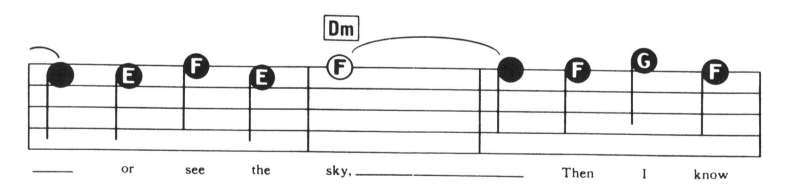

_____ or see the sky, _____ Then I know

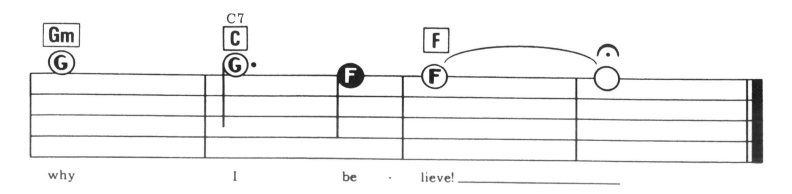

why I be · lieve! _____

I'll Fly Away

Registration 8
Rhythm: Fox Trot

Words and Music by
Albert E. Brumley

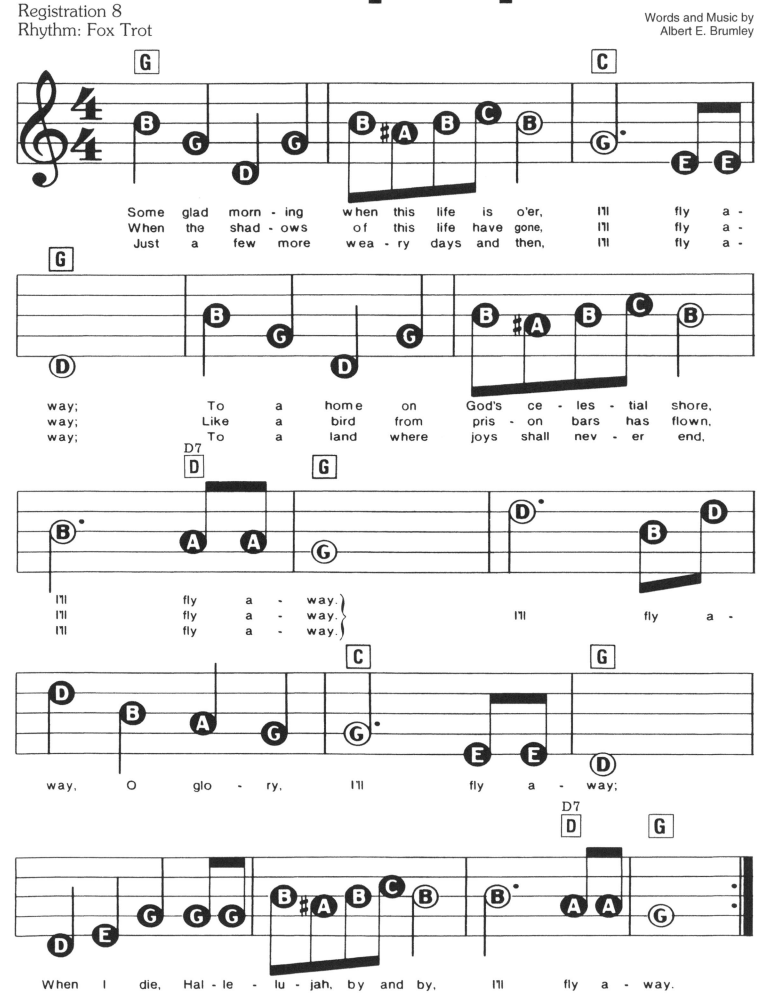

I Saw the Light

Registration 4
Rhythm: Country or Fox Trot

Words and Music by
Hank Williams

23

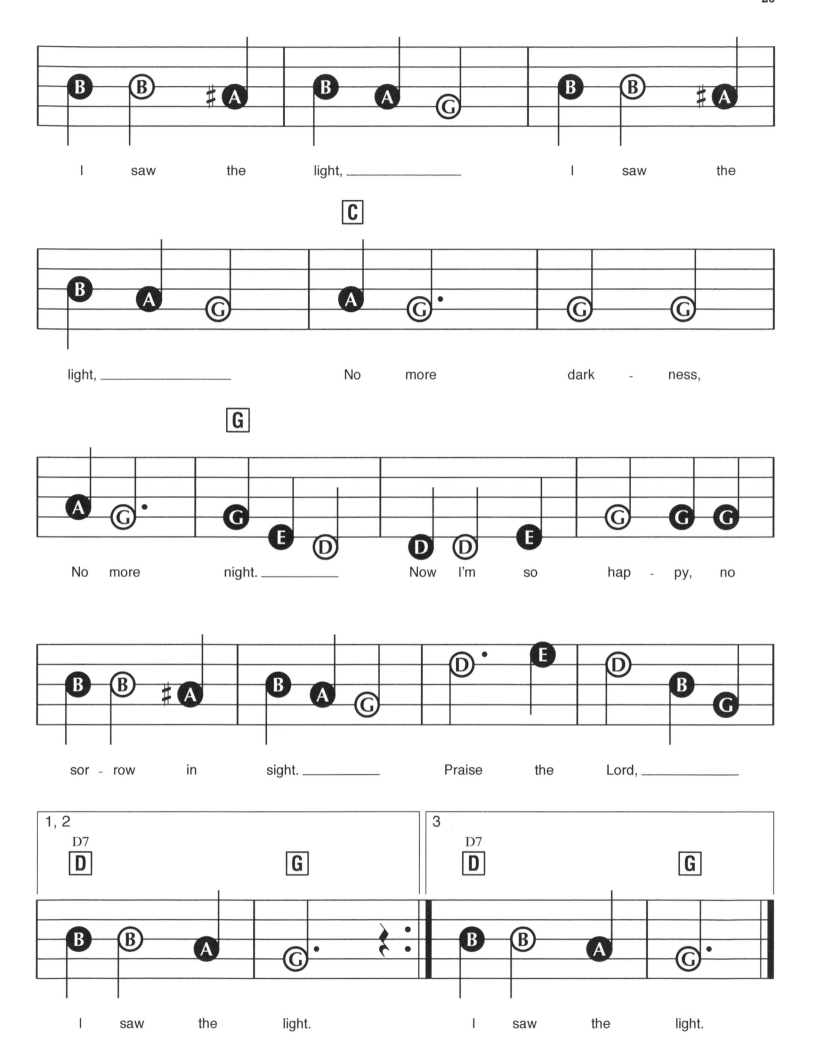

I Will Serve Thee

Registration 3
Rhythm: Fox Trot or March

Words by William J. and Gloria Gaither
Music by William J. Gaither

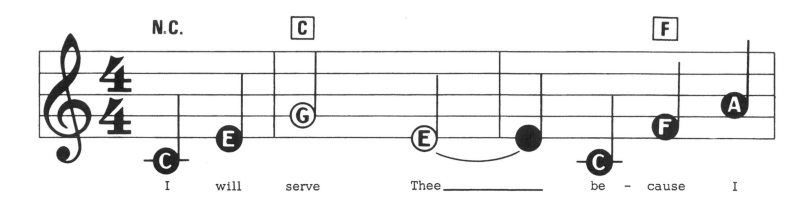

I will serve Thee_____ be - cause I

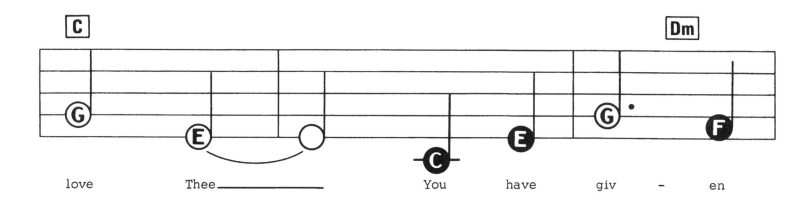

love Thee_____ You have giv - en

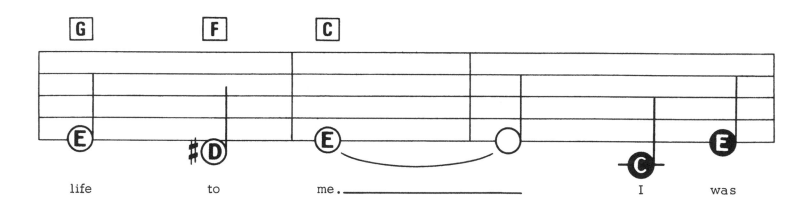

life to me._____ I was

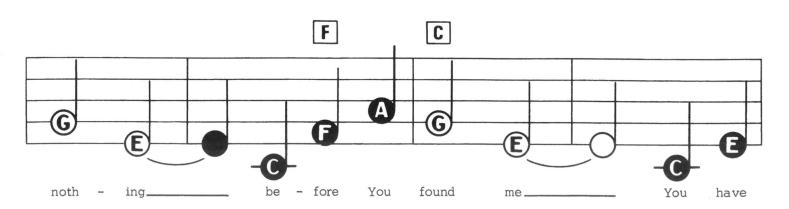

noth - ing_____ be - fore You found me_____ You have

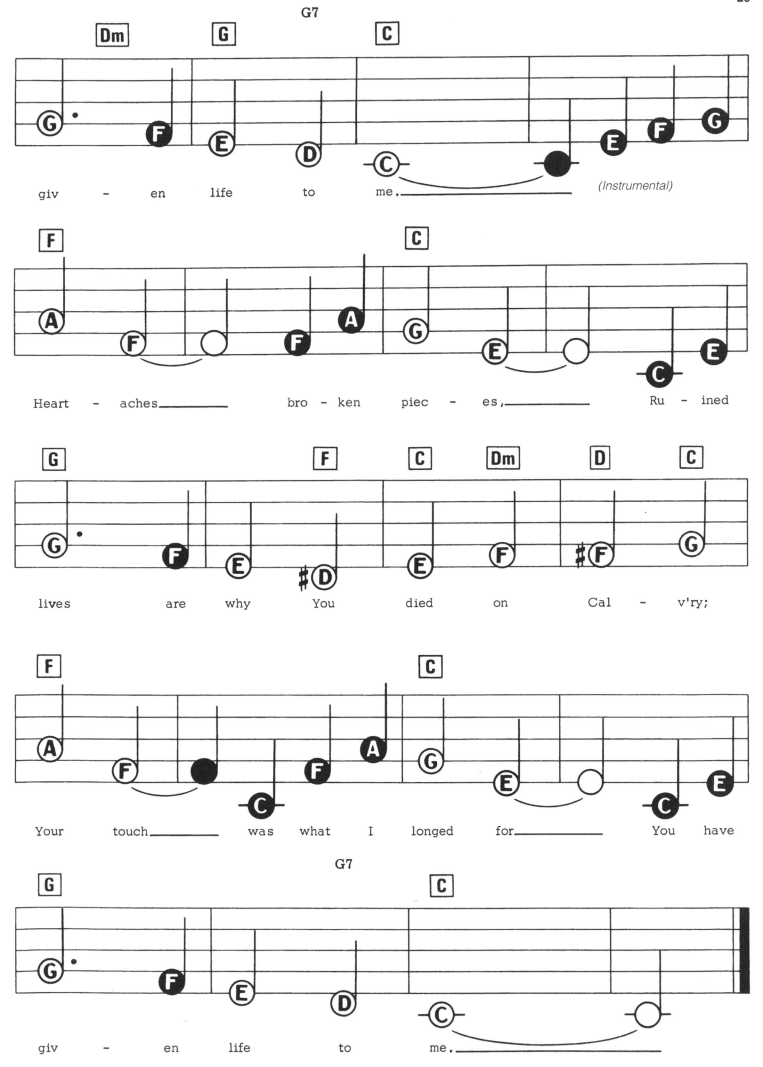

I'd Rather Have Jesus

Registration 8
Rhythm: Waltz

Words by Rhea F. Miller
Music by George Beverly Shea

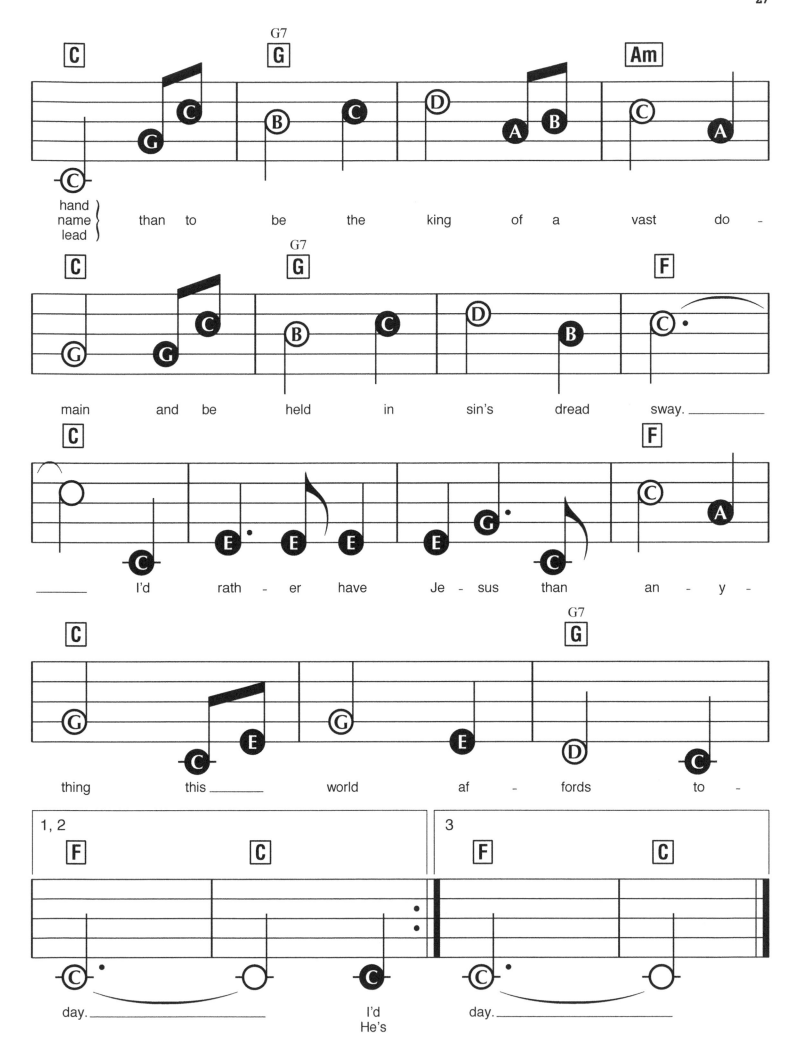

The King Is Coming

Registration 6
Rhythm: Waltz

Words by William J. and Gloria Gaither
and Charles Millhuff
Music by William J. Gaither

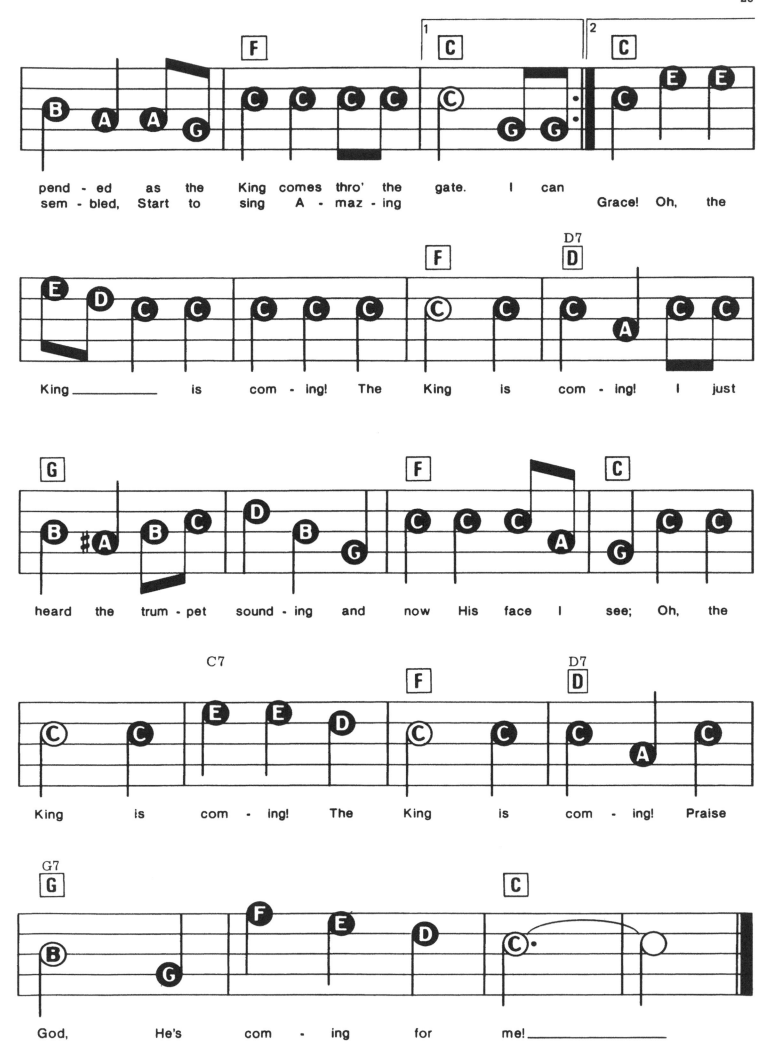

Lead Me, Guide Me

Registration 2
Rhythm: Waltz

Words and Music by
Doris Akers

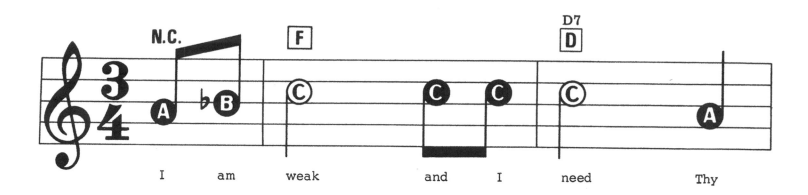

I am weak and I need Thy

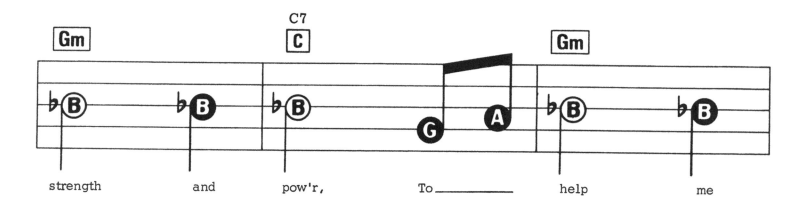

strength and pow'r, To _____ help me

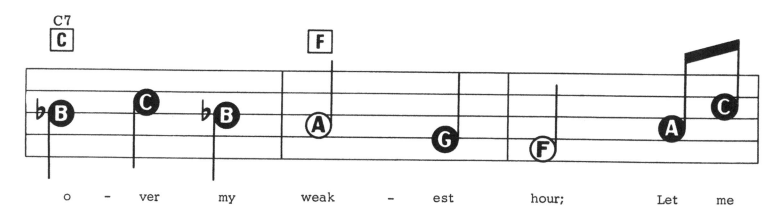

o - ver my weak - est hour; Let me

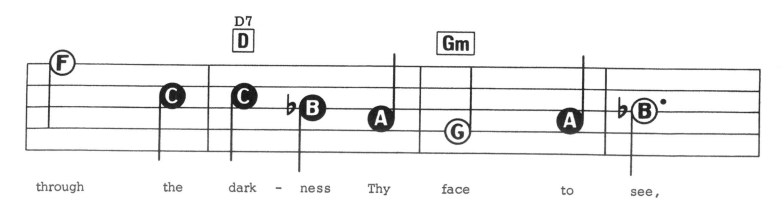

through the dark - ness Thy face to see,

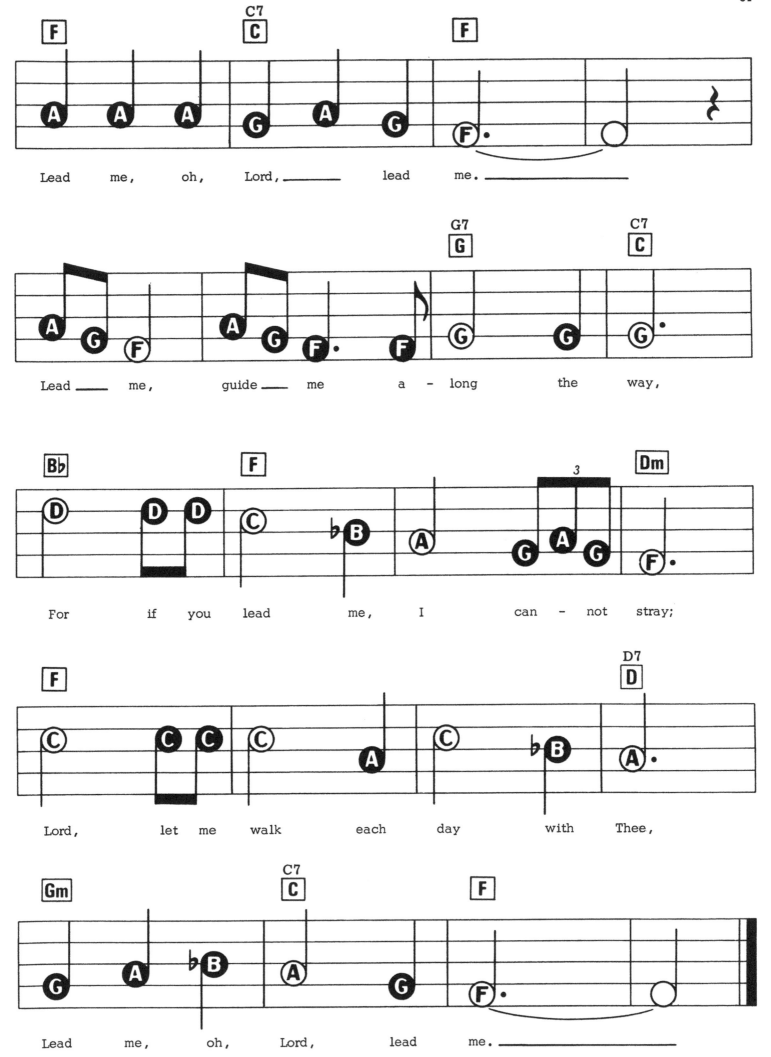

Learning to Lean

Registration 6
Rhythm: Waltz

Words and Music by
John Stallings

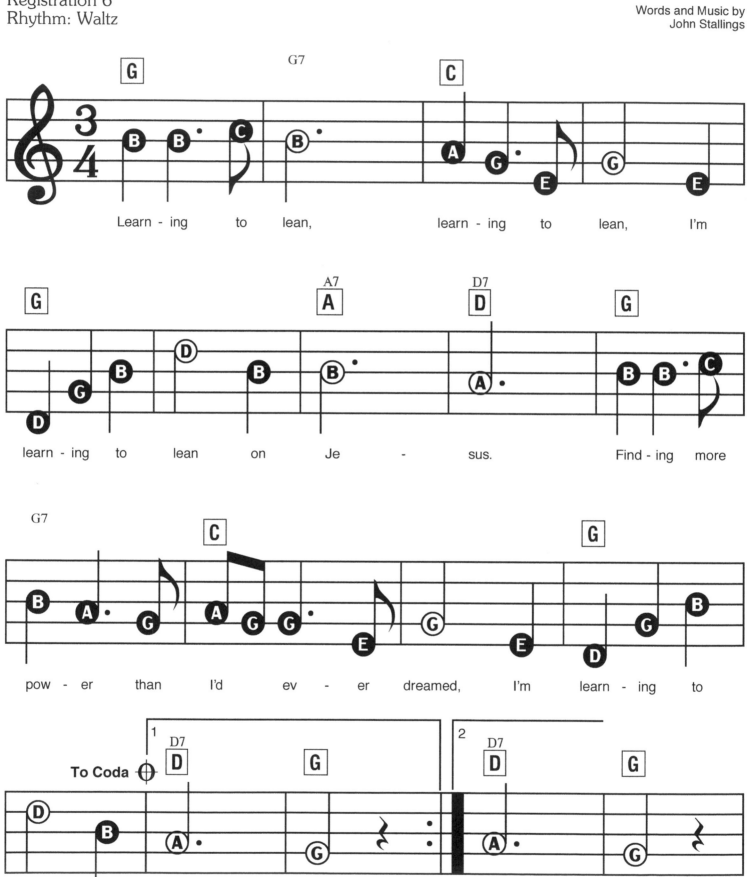

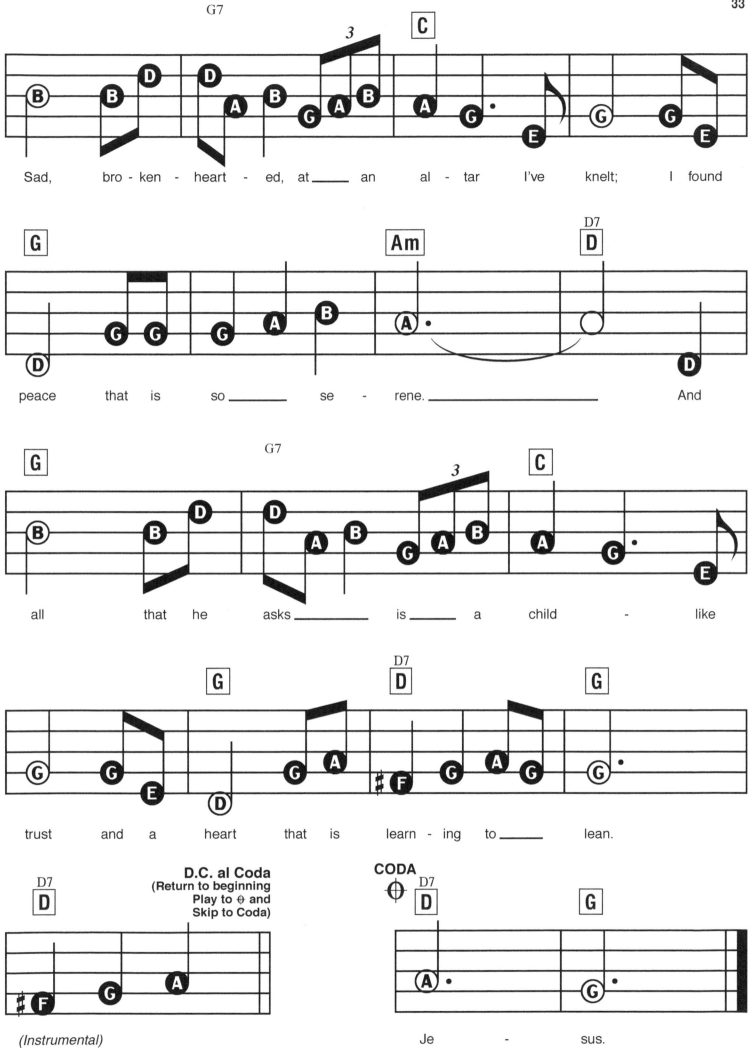

The Longer I Serve Him

Registration 3
Rhythm: Waltz

Words and Music by
William J. Gaither

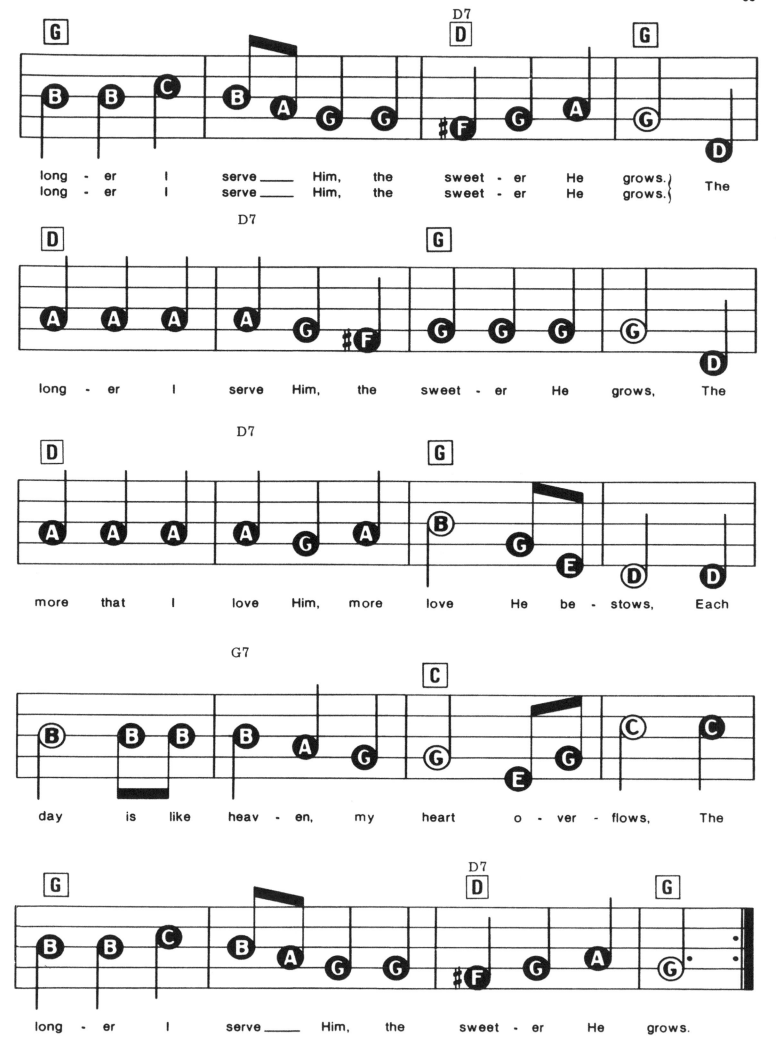

Midnight Cry

Registration 8
Rhythm: 8-Beat or Rock

Words and Music by Greg Day
and Chuck Day

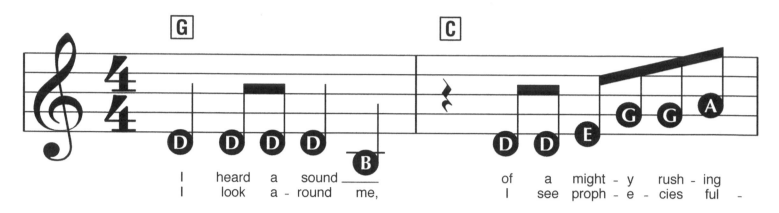

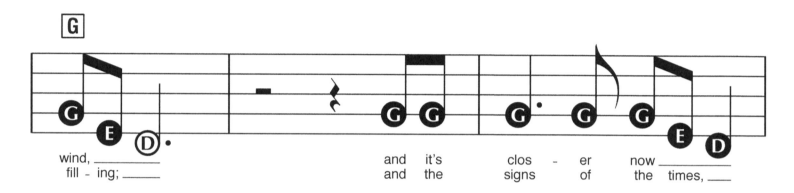

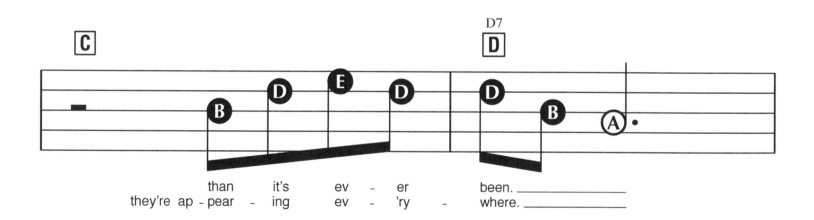

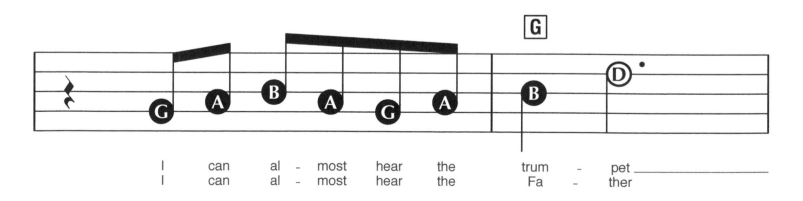

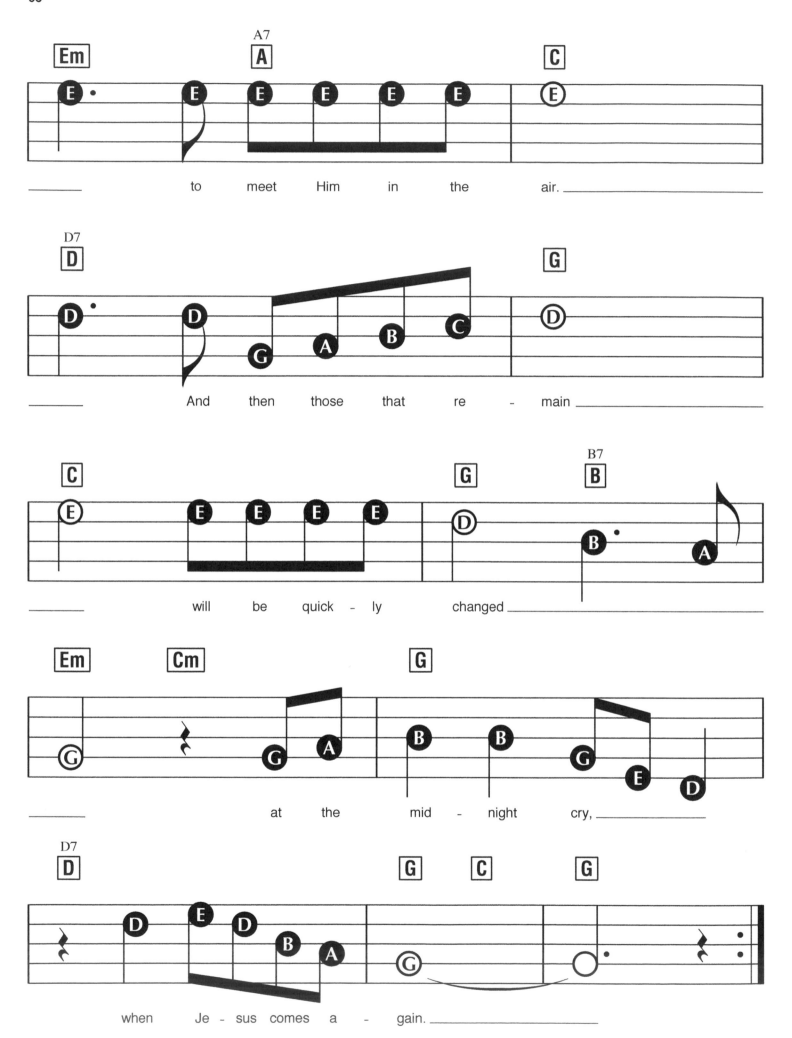

My God Is Real
(Yes, God Is Real)

Registration 2
Rhythm: Slow Rock or Shuffle

Words and Music by
Kenneth Morris

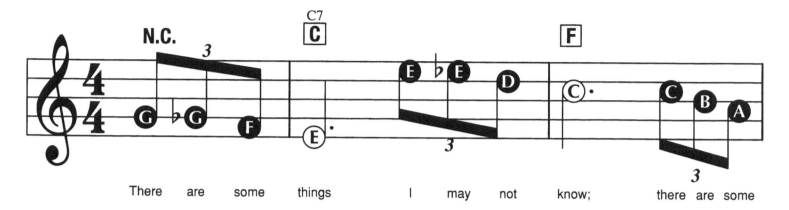

There are some things I may not know; there are some

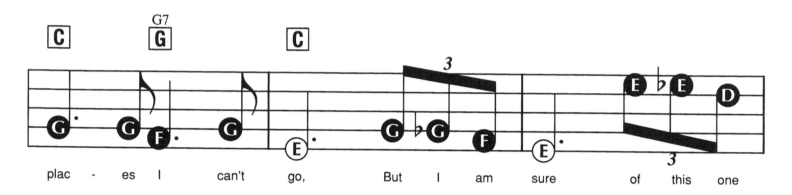

plac - es I can't go, But I am sure of this one

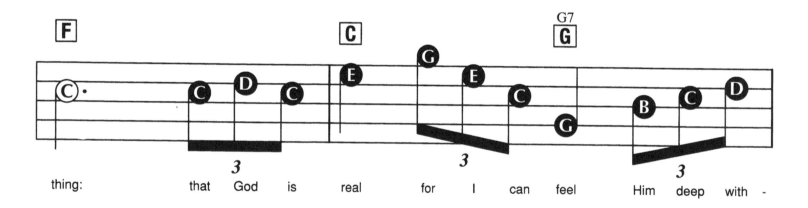

thing: that God is real for I can feel Him deep with -

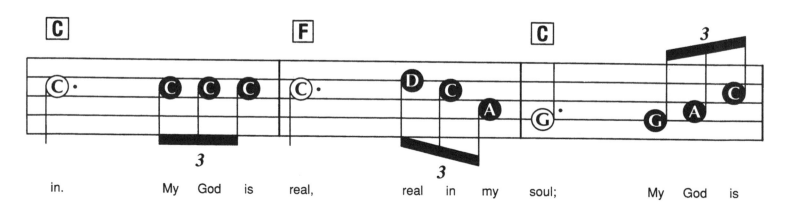

in. My God is real, real in my soul; My God is

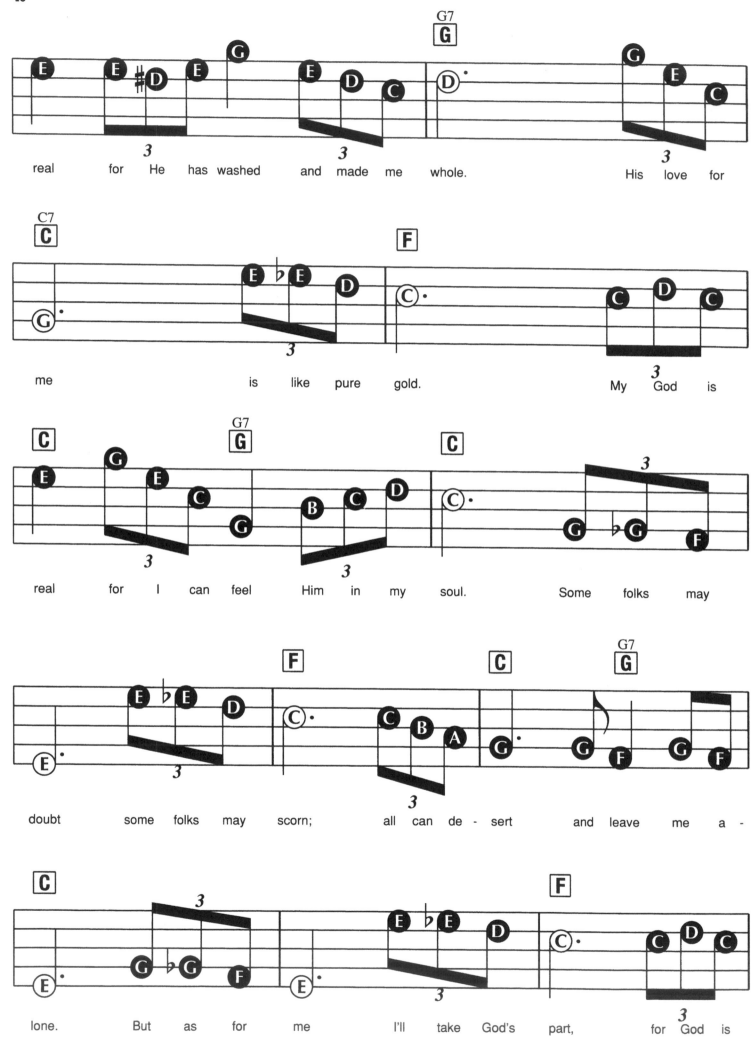

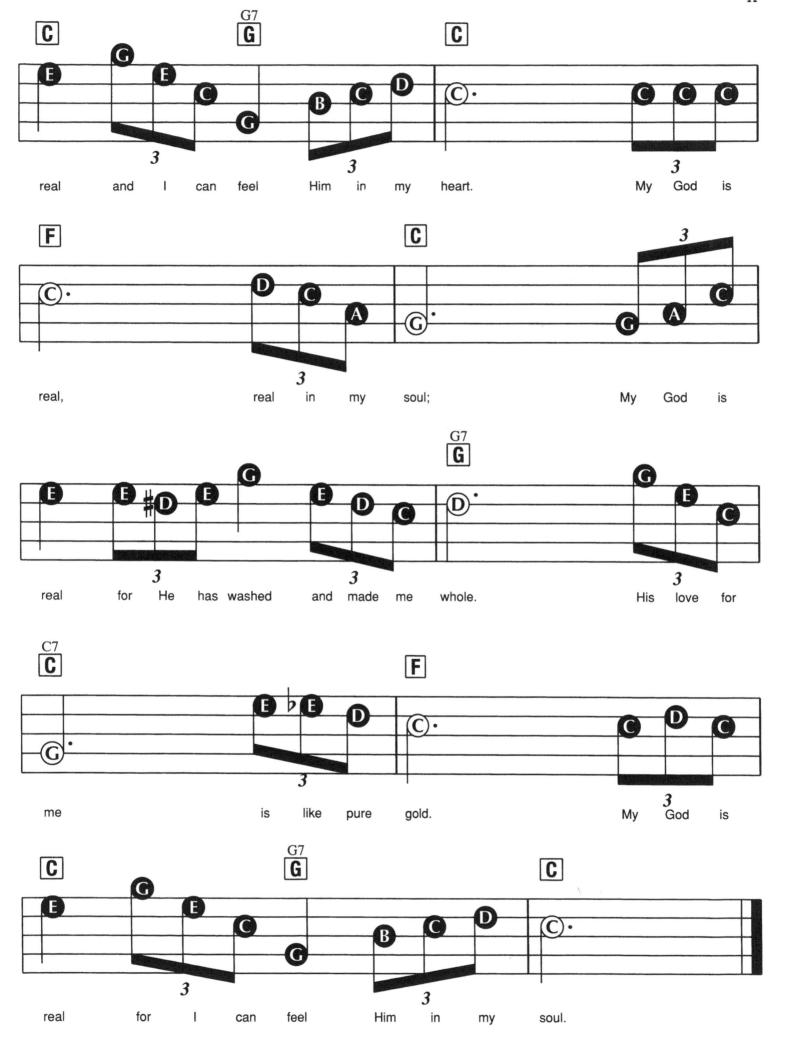

Put Your Hand in the Hand

Registration 4
Rhythm: Rock or Jazz Rock

Words and Music by
Gene MacLellan

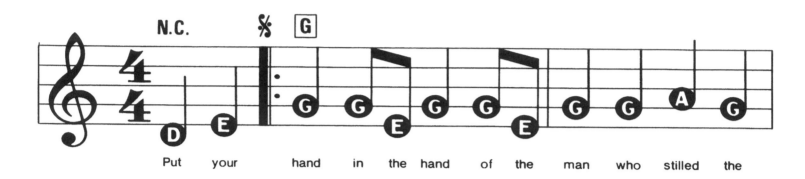

Put your hand in the hand of the man who stilled the

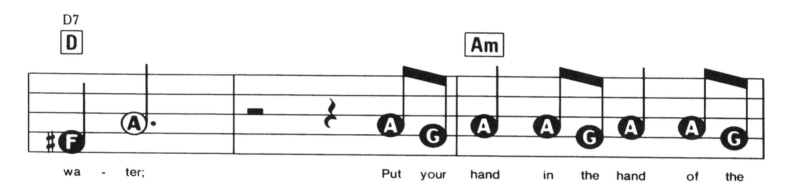

wa - ter; Put your hand in the hand of the

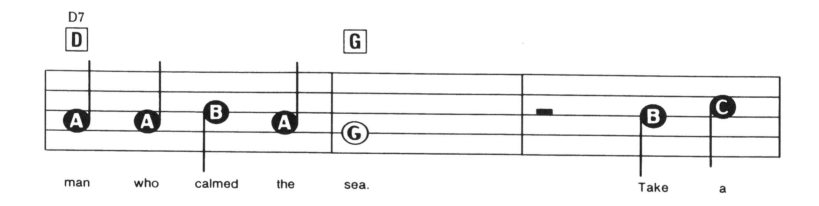

man who calmed the sea. Take a

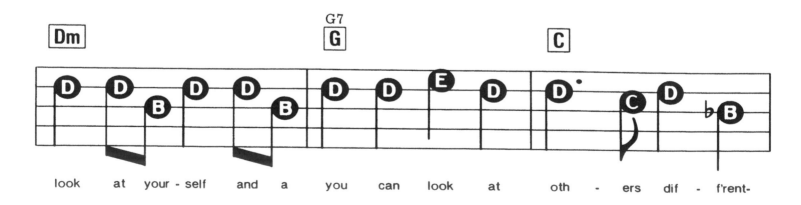

look at your - self and a you can look at oth - ers dif - f'rent-

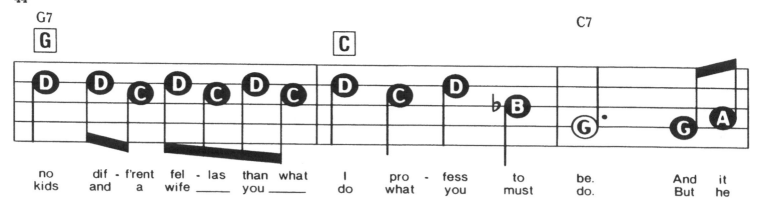

no dif - f'rent fel - las than what I pro - fess to be. And it
kids and a wife _____ you _____ do what you to must do. But he

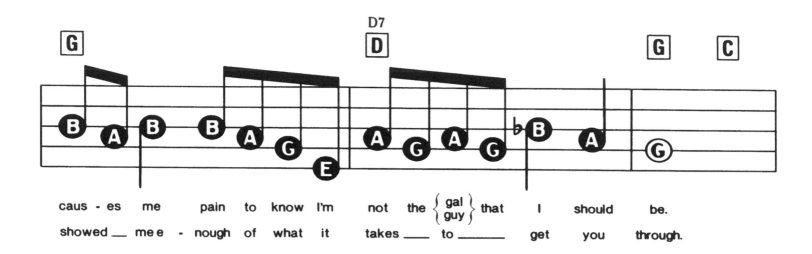

caus - es me pain to know I'm not the { gal / guy } that I should be.
showed _ me e - nough of what it takes ___ to _____ get you through.

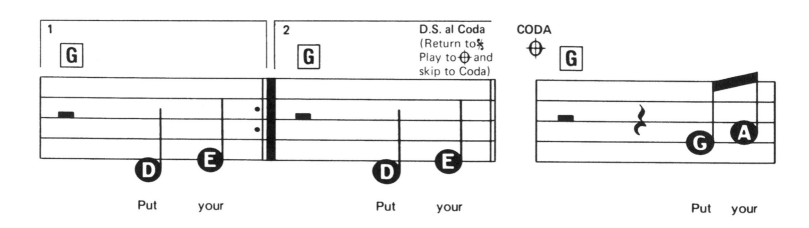

1 — Put your
2 — D.S. al Coda (Return to % Play to ⊕ and skip to Coda) — Put your
CODA — Put your

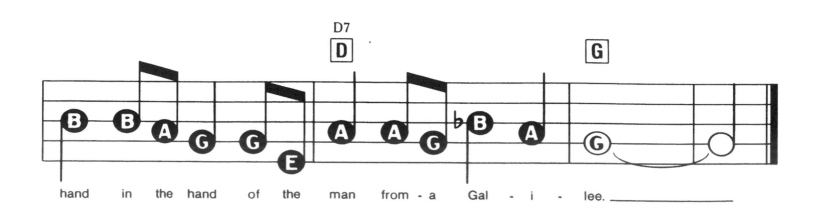

hand in the hand of the man from - a Gal - i - lee. _____

Reach Out to Jesus

Registration 7
Rhythm: Waltz

Words and Music by
Ralph Carmichael

Is your bur - den heav - y as you bear it all a -
Is the life you're liv - ing filled with sor - row and de -

lone? _____ Does the road you trav - el har - bor
spair? _____ Does the fu - ture press you with its

dan - gers yet un - known? _____ Are you grow - ing
wor - ry and its care? _____ Are you tired and

wea - ry in the strug - gle of it all? _____
friend - less, have you al - most lost your way? _____

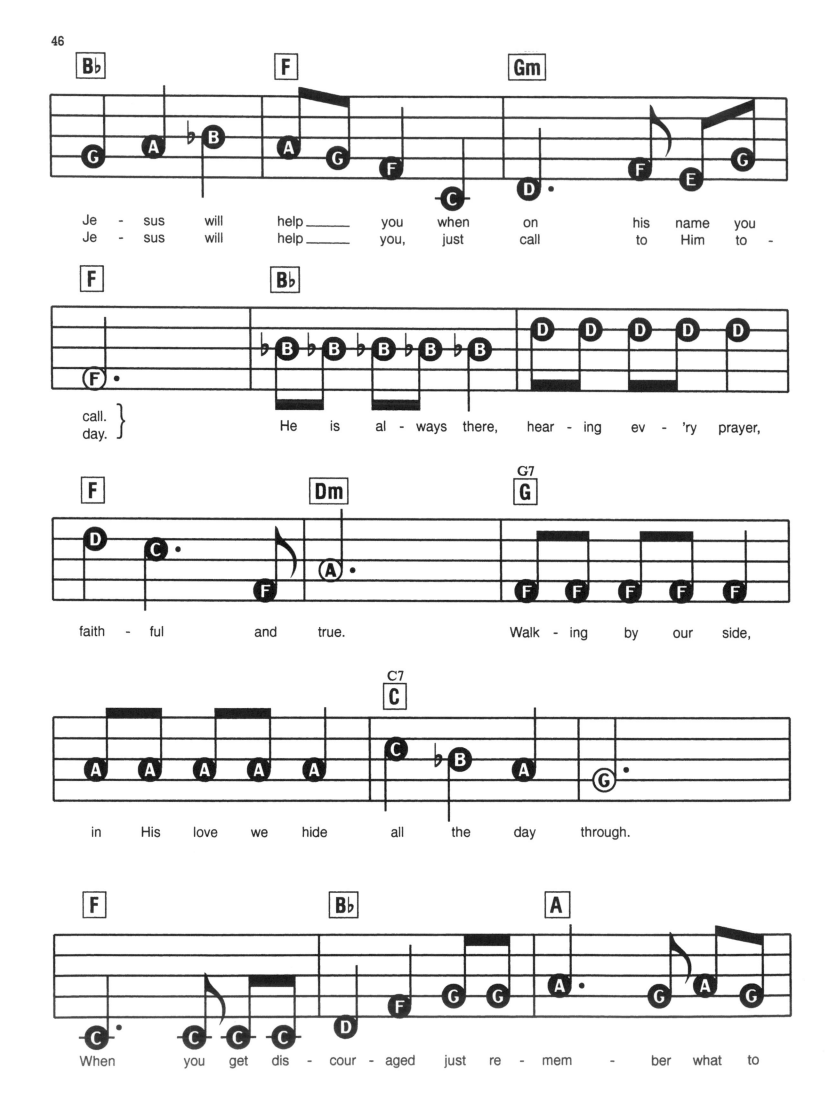

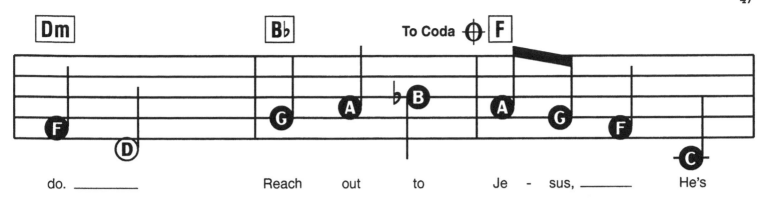

do. _____ Reach out to Je - sus, _____ He's

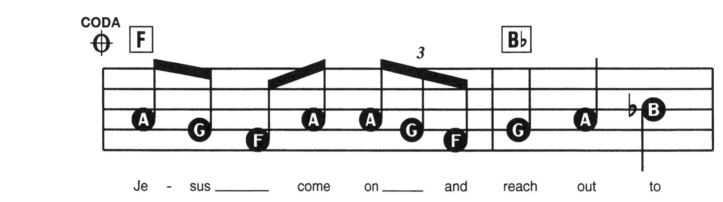

reach - ing out to you.

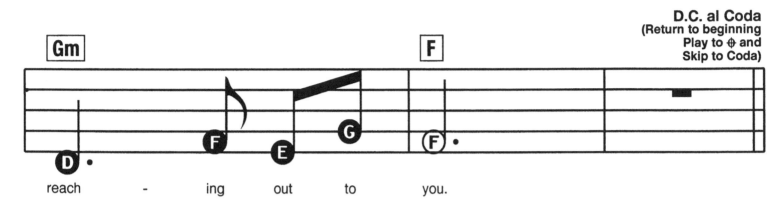

Je - sus _____ come on ____ and reach out to

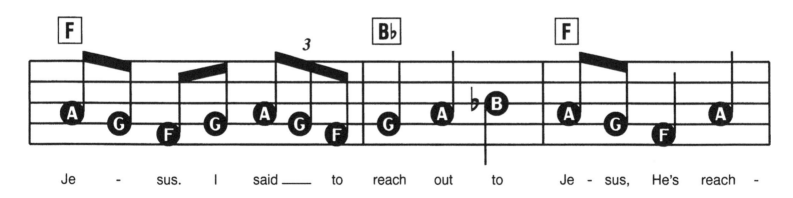

Je - sus. I said ____ to reach out to Je - sus, He's reach -

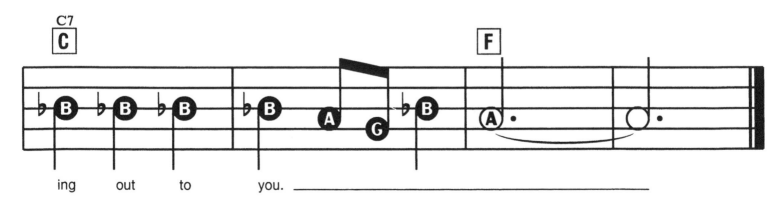

ing out to you. _____

The Robe of Calvary

Registration 4
Rhythm: March

Words and Music by Fred Wise,
Benjamin Weisman, Kay Twomey
and Elaine Rivers

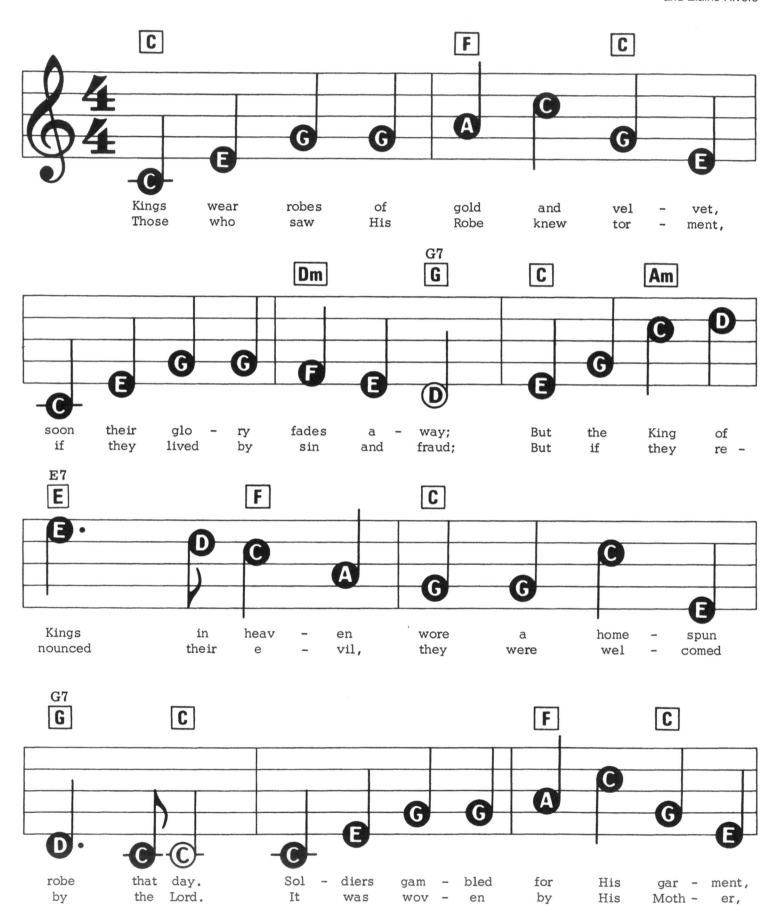

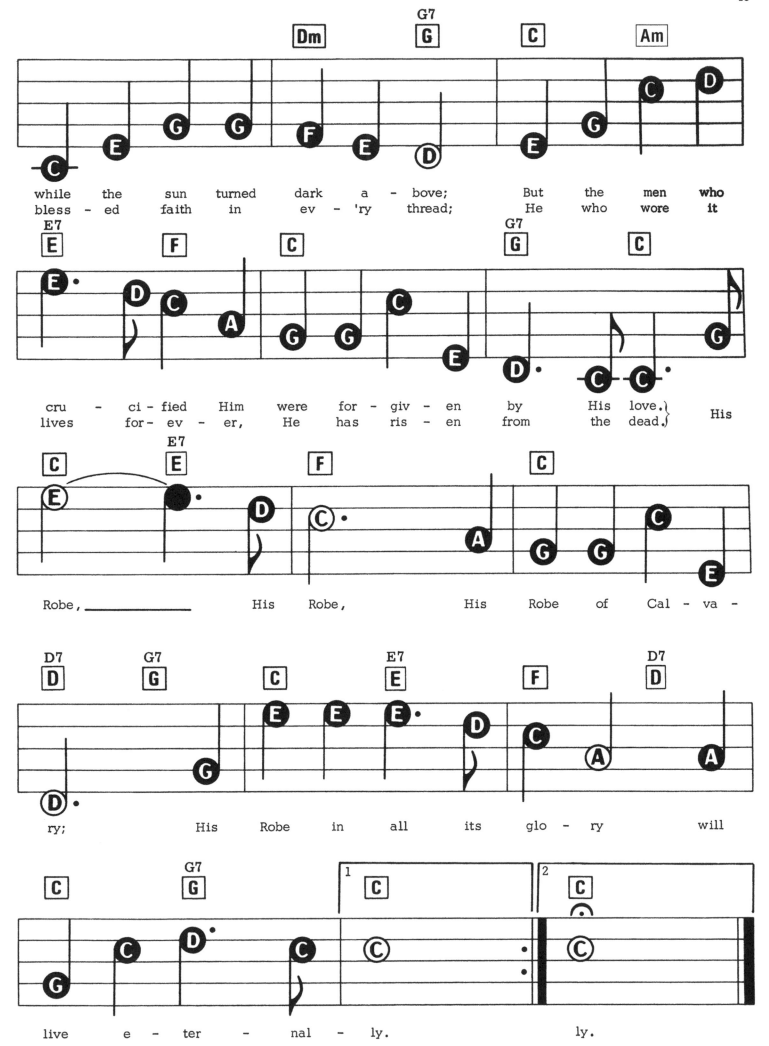

Room at the Cross for You

Registration 6
Rhythm: Waltz

Words and Music by
Ira F. Stanphill

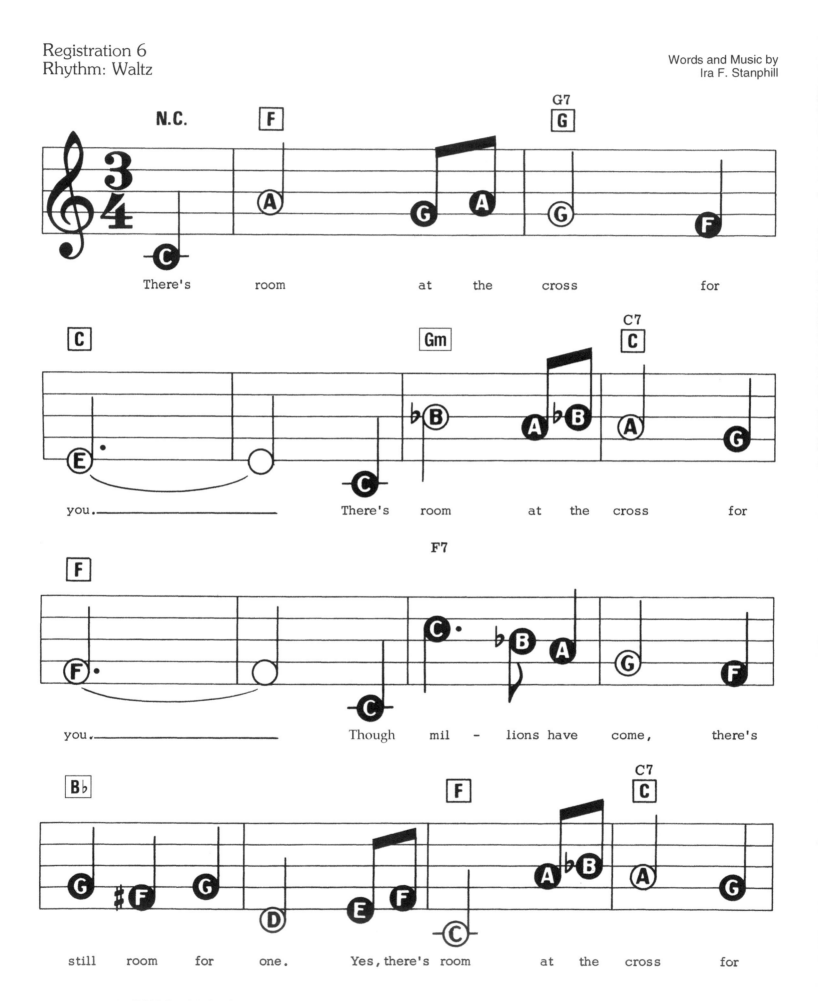

There's room at the cross for you.____ There's room at the cross for you.____ Though mil - lions have come, there's still room for one. Yes, there's room at the cross for

51

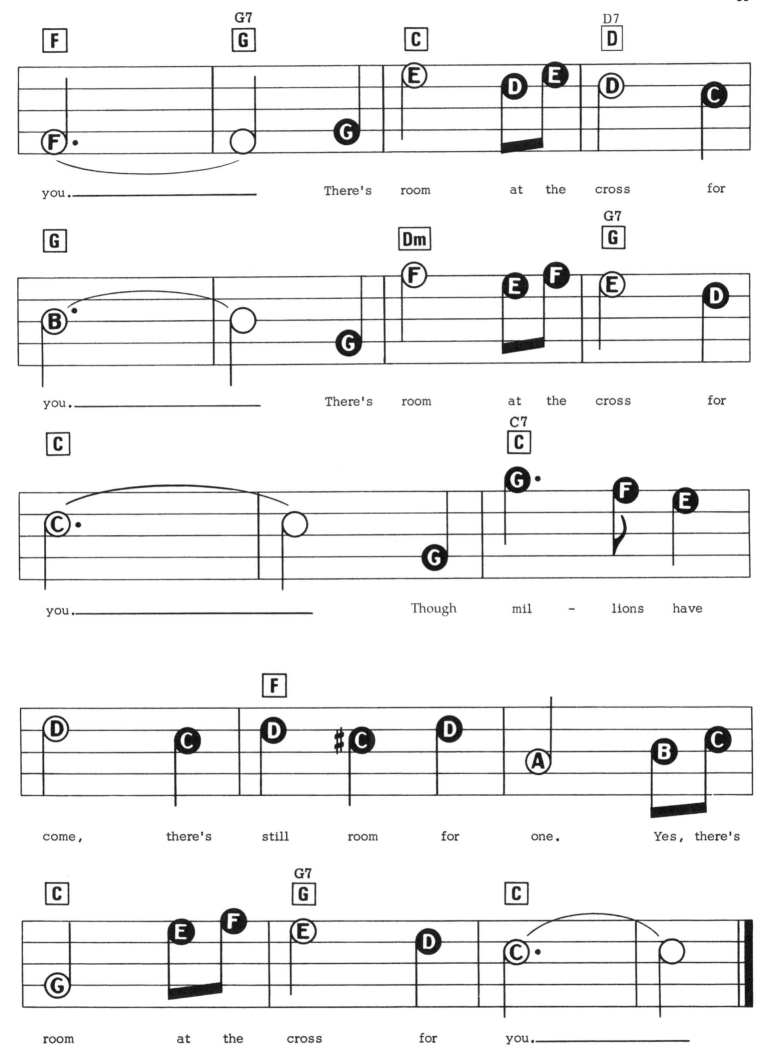

Sheltered in the Arms of God

Registration 8
Rhythm: 4/4 Ballad or Fox Trot

Words and Music by Dottie Rambo
and Jimmie Davis

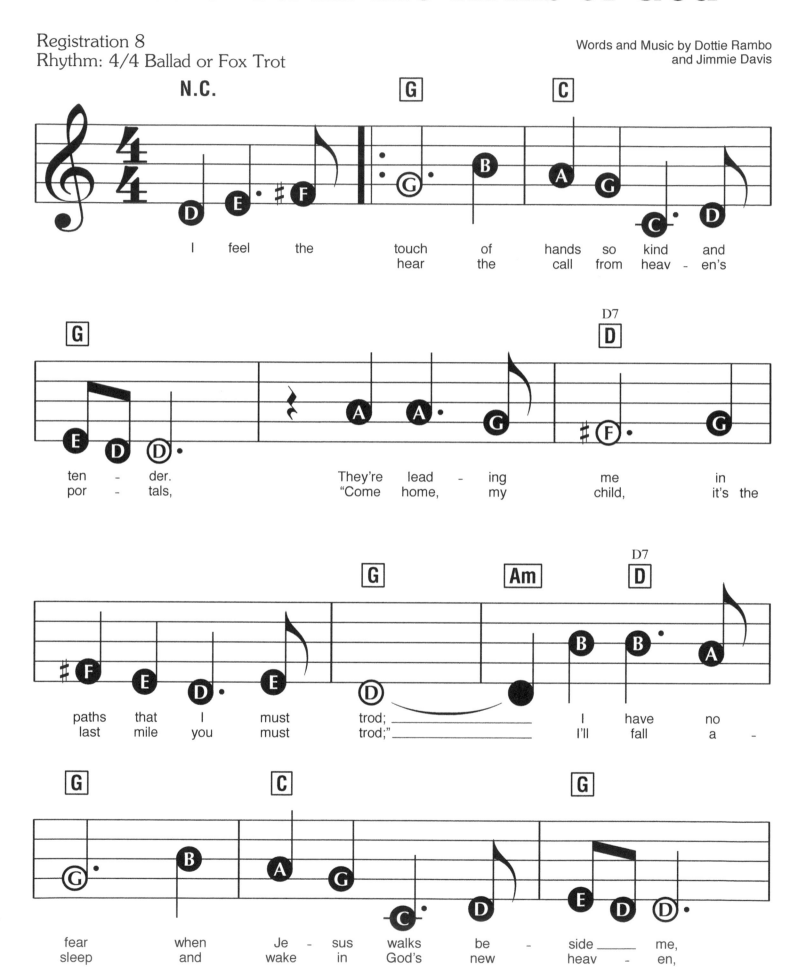

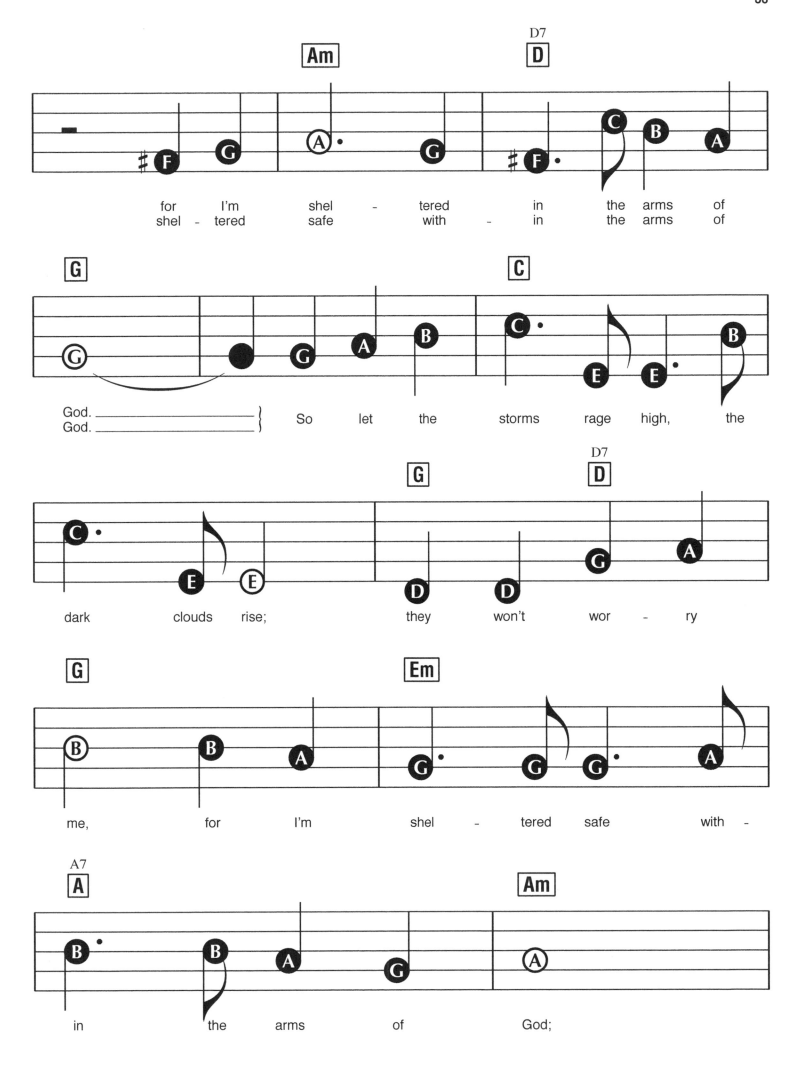

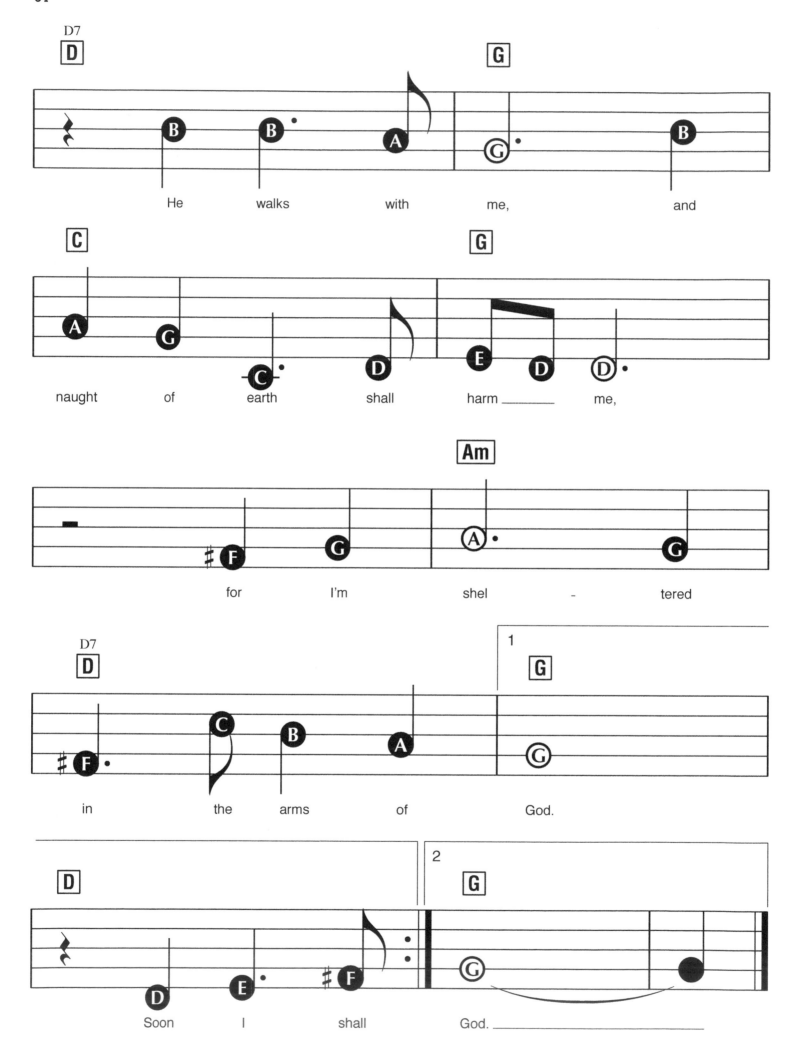

Step Into the Water

Registration 8
Rhythm: Fox Trot

Words and Music by
L. Kirk Talley

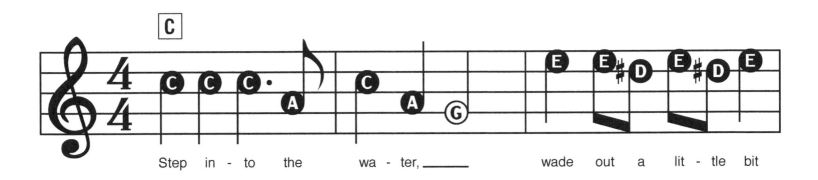

Step in-to the wa-ter, _____ wade out a lit-tle bit

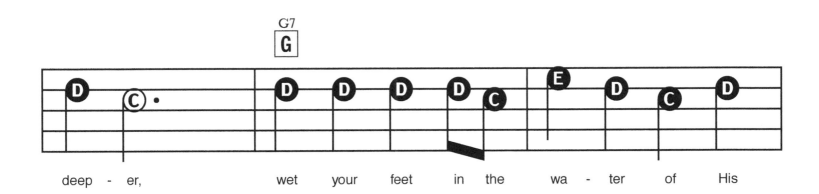

deep-er, wet your feet in the wa-ter of His

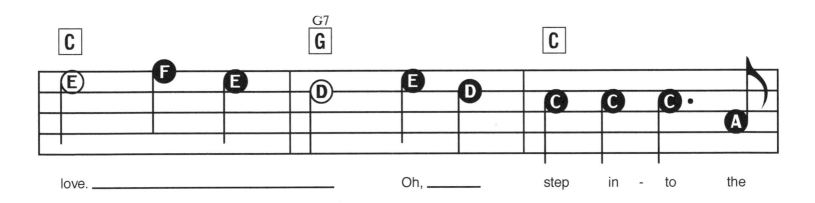

love. _____ Oh, _____ step in-to the

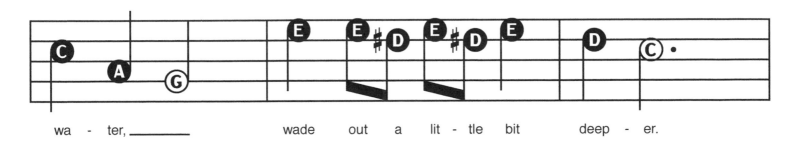

wa-ter, _____ wade out a lit-tle bit deep-er.

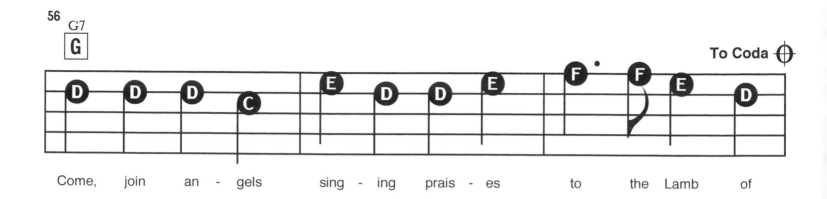

To Coda ⊕

Come, join an - gels sing - ing prais - es to the Lamb of

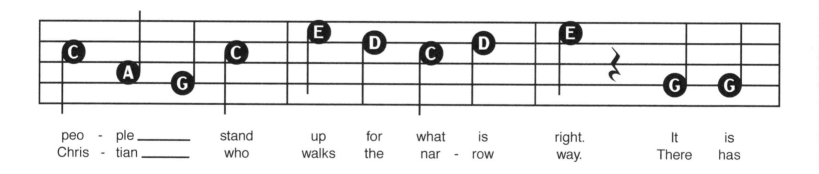

God. _____

{ It is time we the
{ There is vic - t'ry for the

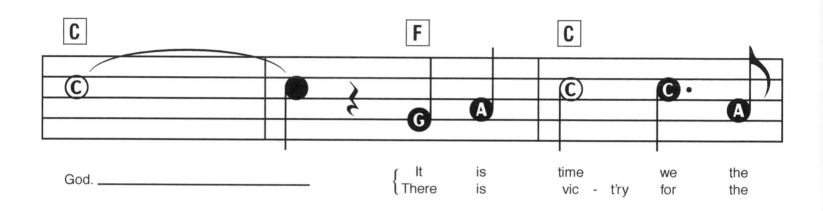

peo - ple ____ stand up for what is right. It is
Chris - tian ____ who walks the nar - row way. There has

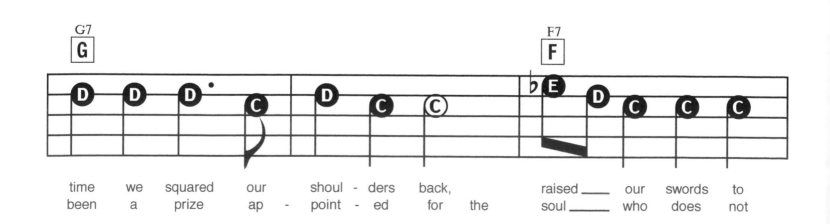

time we squared our shoul - ders back, raised ____ our swords to
been a prize ap - point - ed for the soul ____ who does not

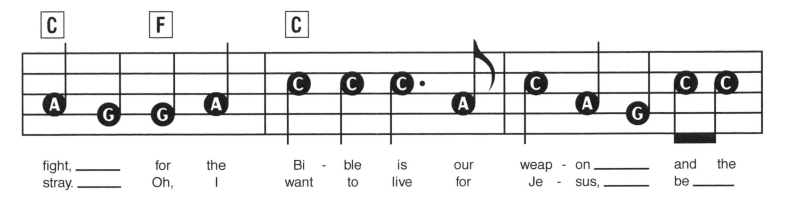

fight, _____ for the Bi - ble is our weap - on _____ and the
stray. _____ Oh, I want to live for Je - sus, _____ be _____

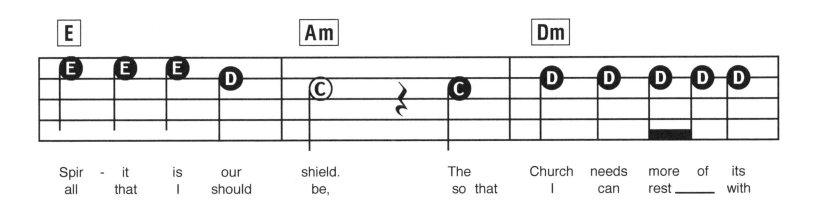

Spir - it is our shield. The Church needs more of its
all that I should be, so that I can rest _____ with

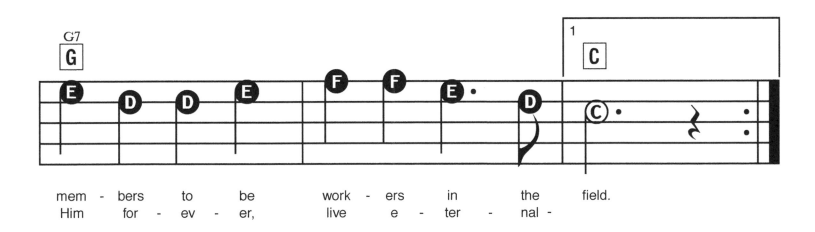

mem - bers to be work - ers in the field.
Him for - ev - er, live e - ter - nal -

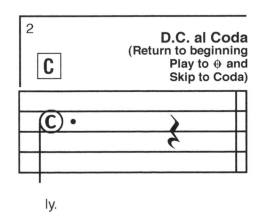

ly.

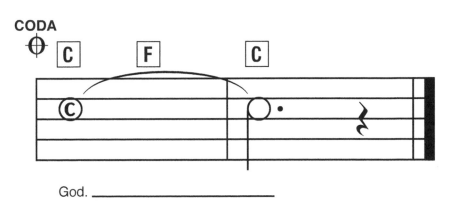

God. _____

Someday There'll Be No Tomorrow

Registration 2
Rhythm: Waltz

Words and Music by
Jenny Lou Carson

Something Beautiful

Registration 3
Rhythm: Swing

Words by Gloria Gaither
Music by William J. Gaither

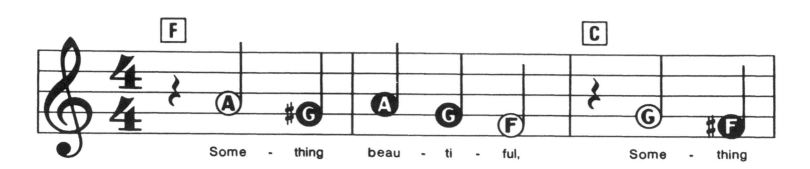

Some - thing beau - ti - ful, Some - thing

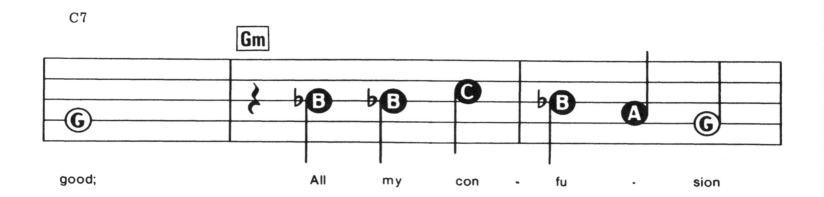

good; All my con - fu - sion

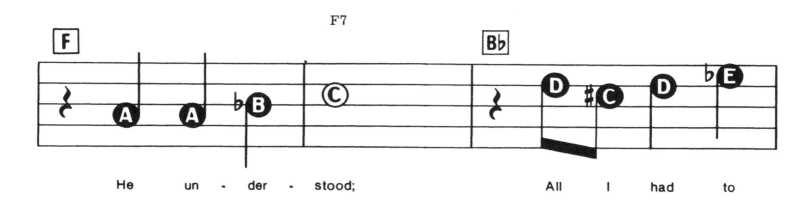

He un - der - stood; All I had to

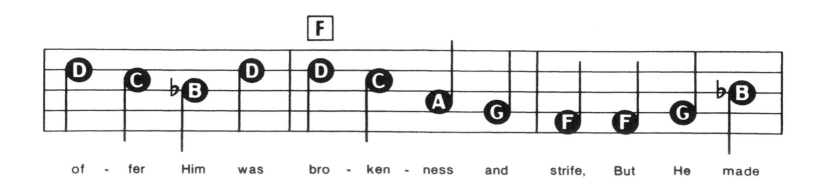

of - fer Him was bro - ken - ness and strife, But He made

some - thing beau - ti - ful of my life.

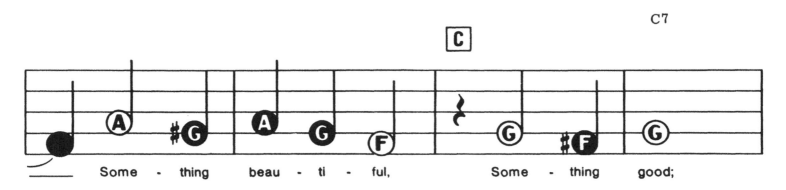

Some - thing beau - ti - ful, Some - thing good;

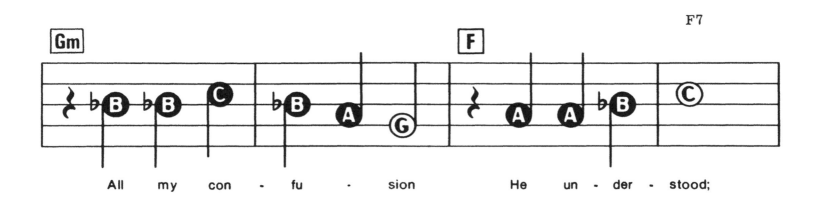

All my con - fu - sion He un - der - stood;

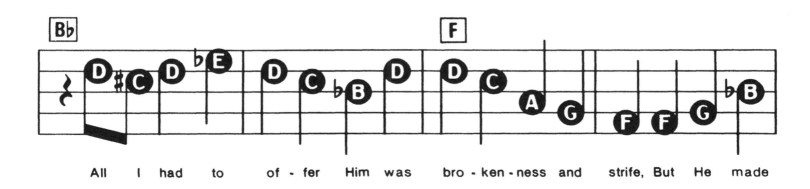

All I had to of - fer Him was bro - ken - ness and strife, But He made

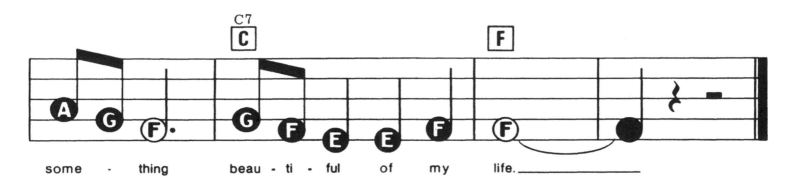

some - thing beau - ti - ful of my life.

Soon and Very Soon

Registration 8
Rhythm: Soul or Fox Trot

Words and Music by
Andraé Crouch

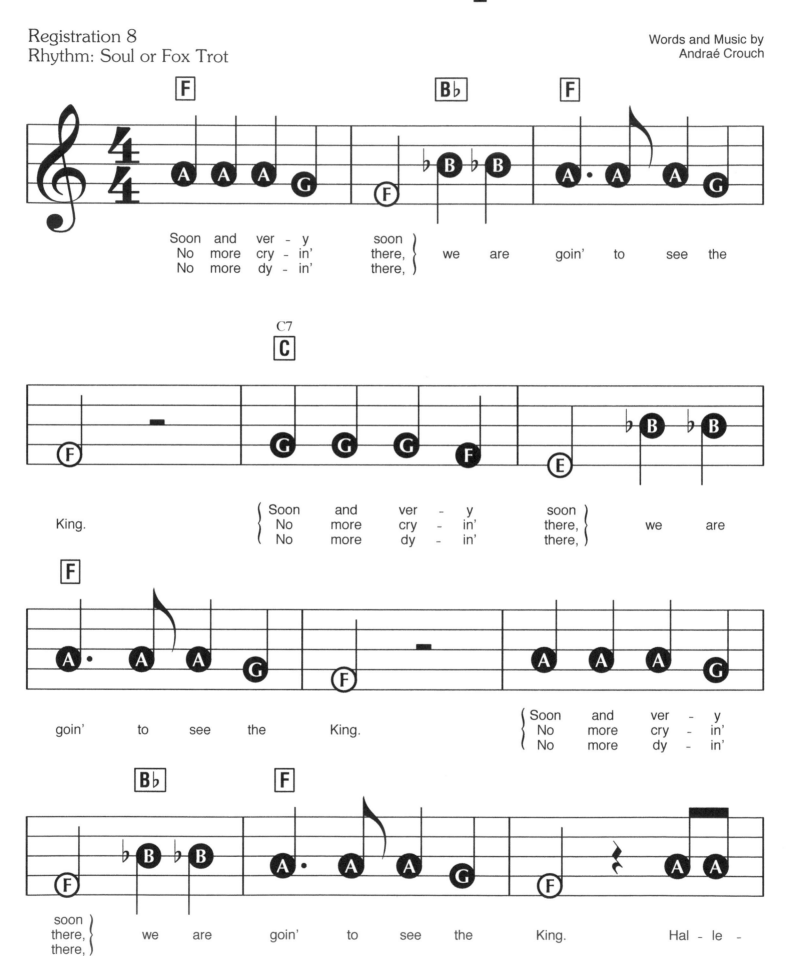

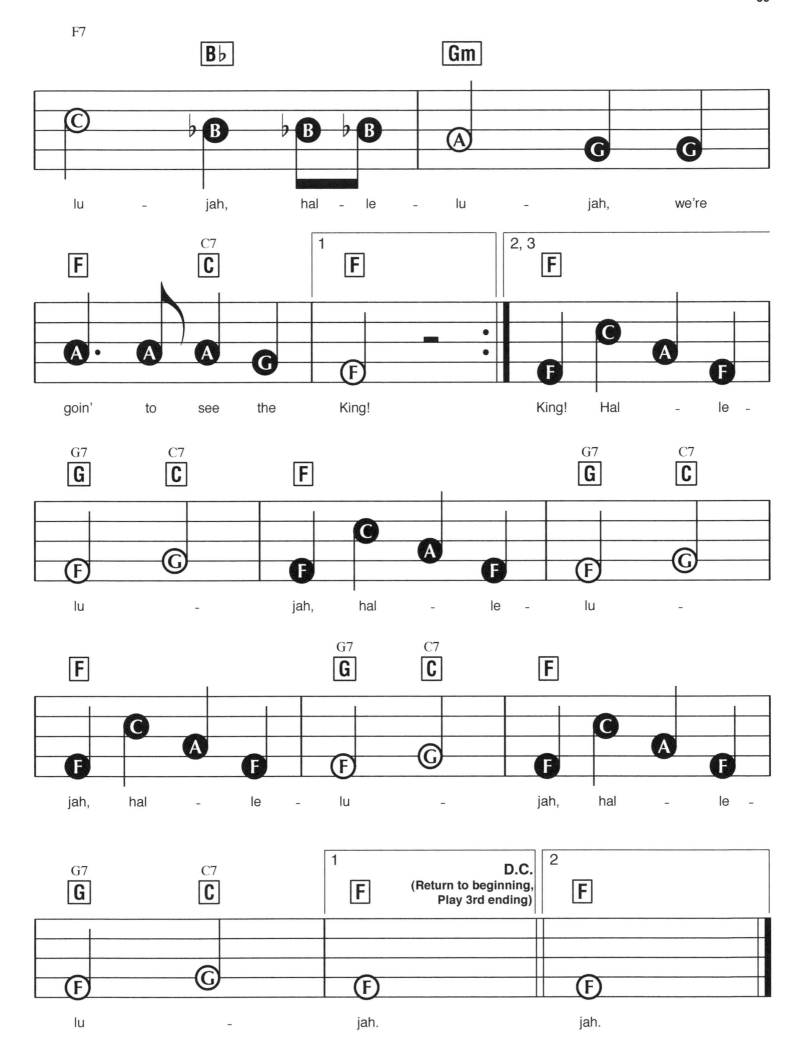

Suppertime

Registration 5
Rhythm: Ballad

Words and Music by
Ira F. Stanphill

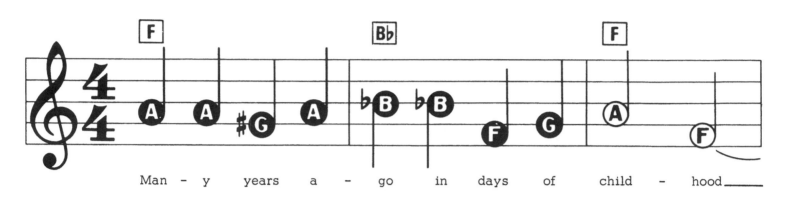

Man - y years a - go in days of child - hood

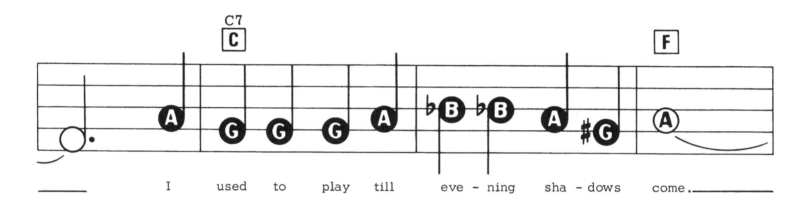

I used to play till eve - ning sha - dows come.

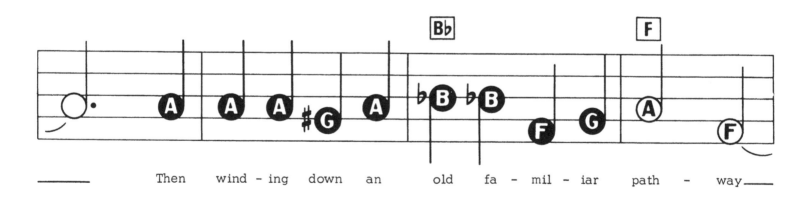

Then wind - ing down an old fa - mil - iar path - way

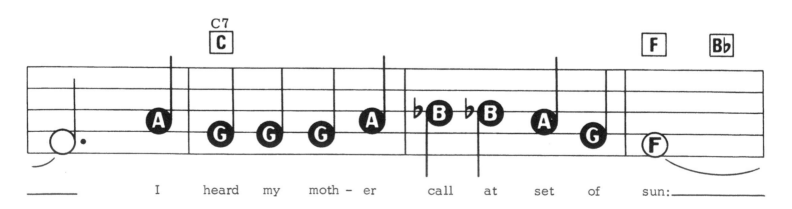

I heard my moth - er call at set of sun:

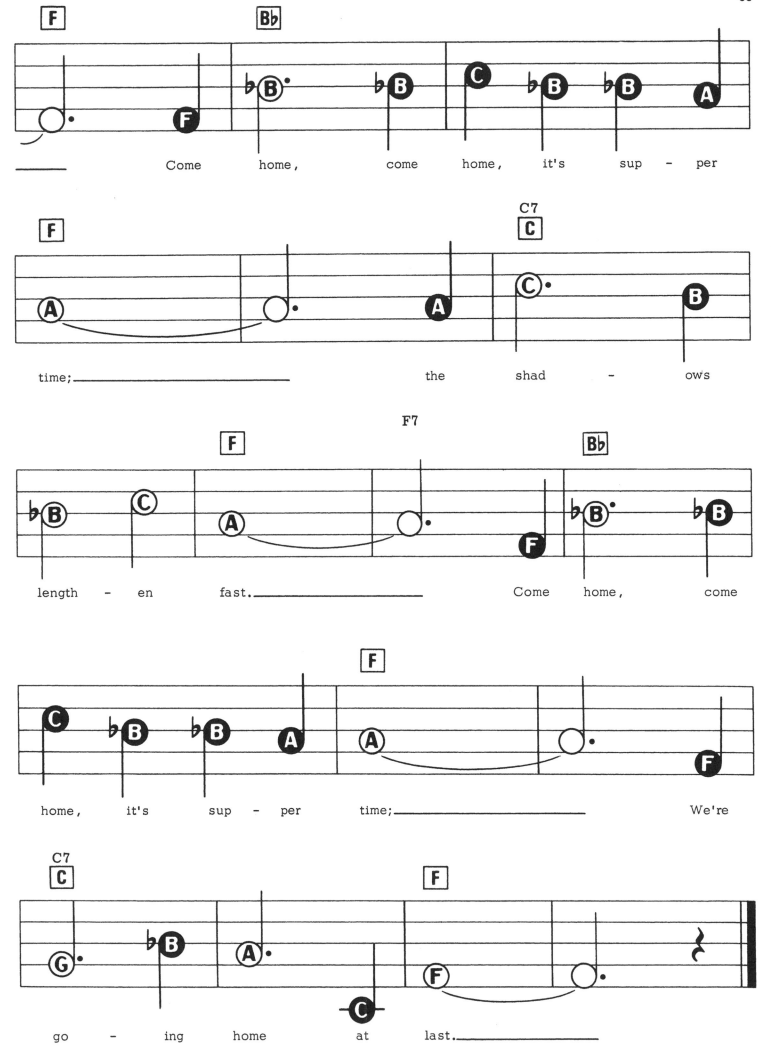

Surely the Presence
of the Lord Is in This Place

Registration 2
Rhythm: Waltz

Words and Music by
Lanny Wolfe

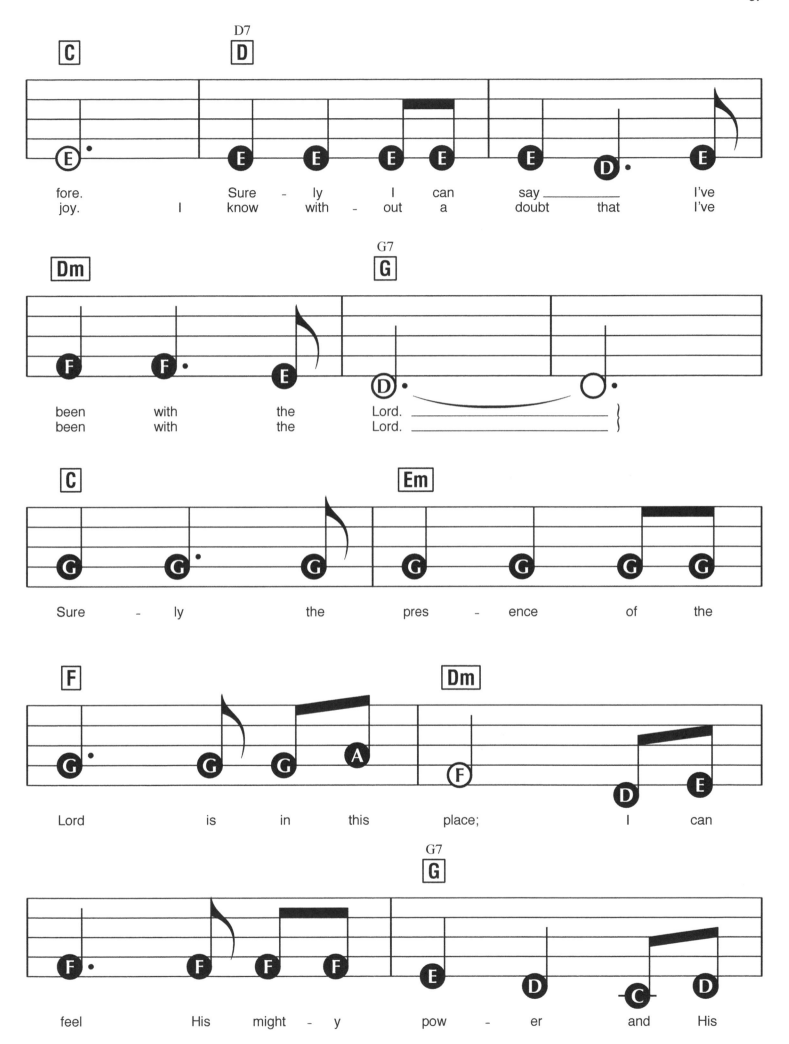

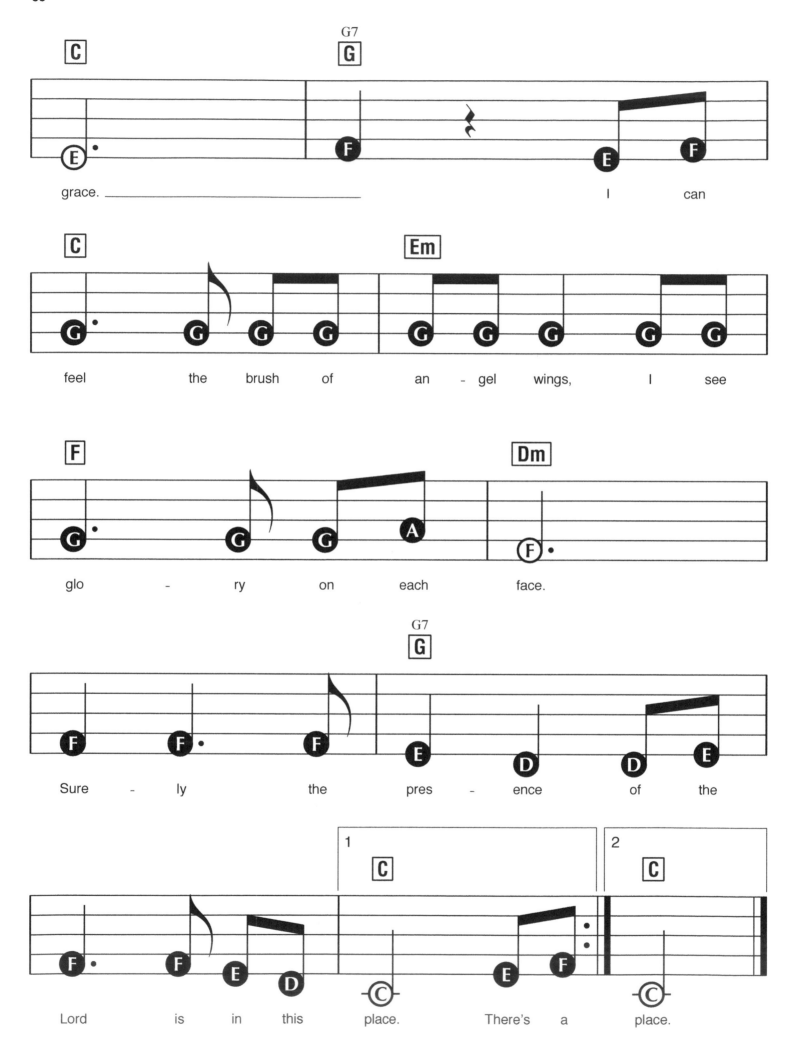

Triumphantly, the Church Will Rise

Registration 7
Rhythm: Waltz or None

Words and Music by
Kirk Talley

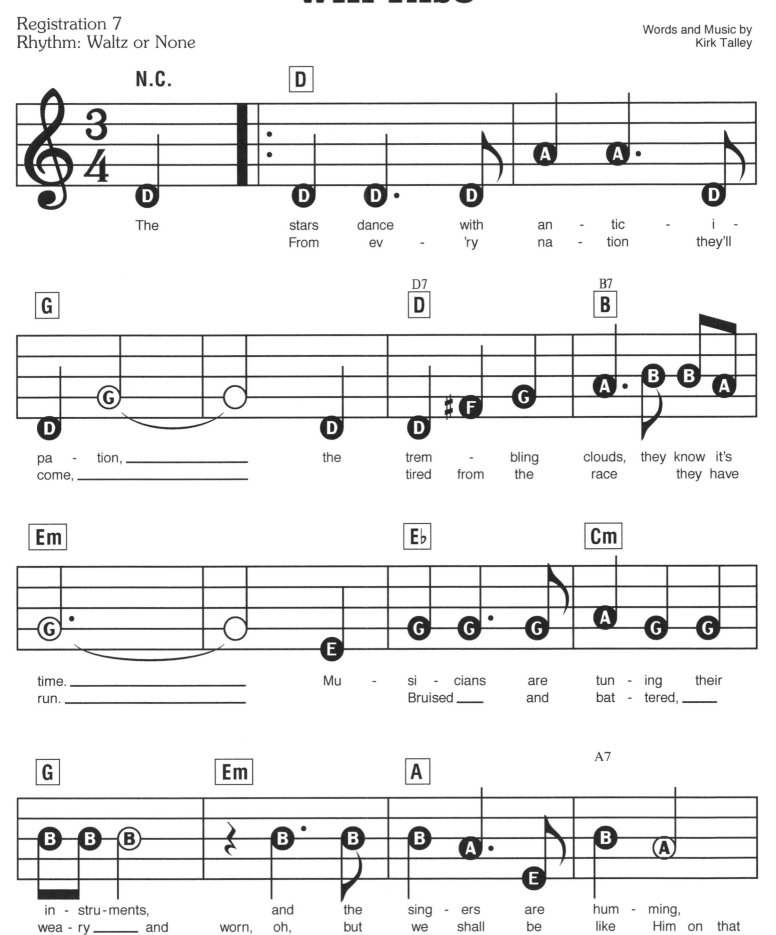

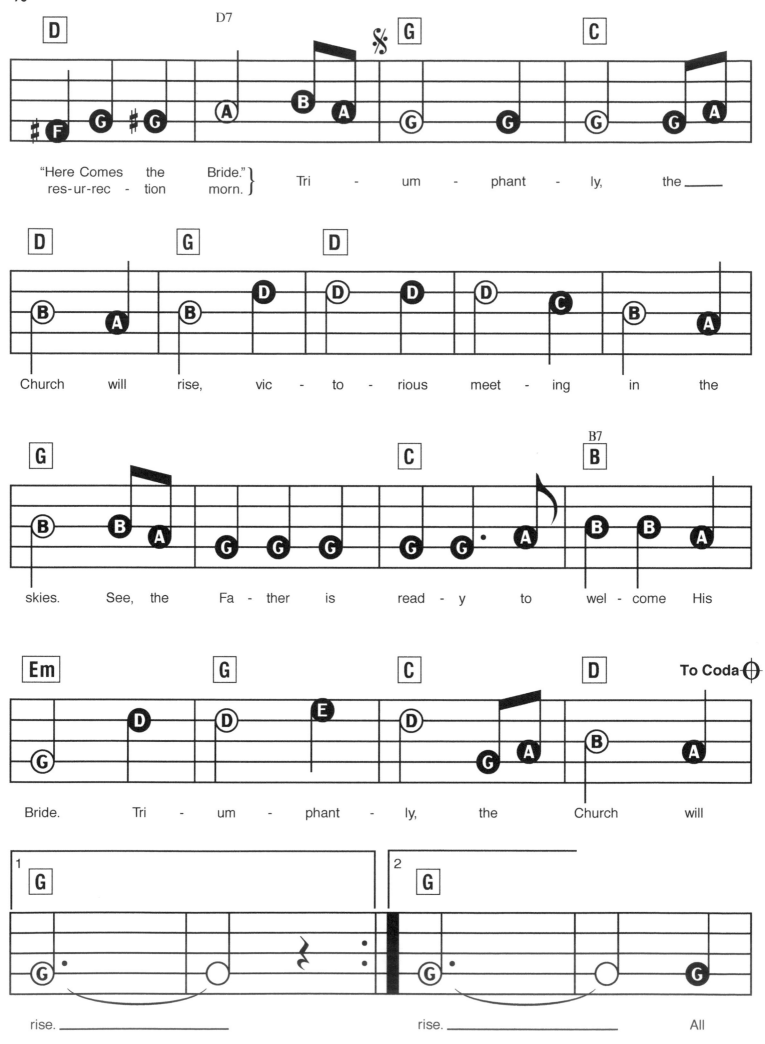

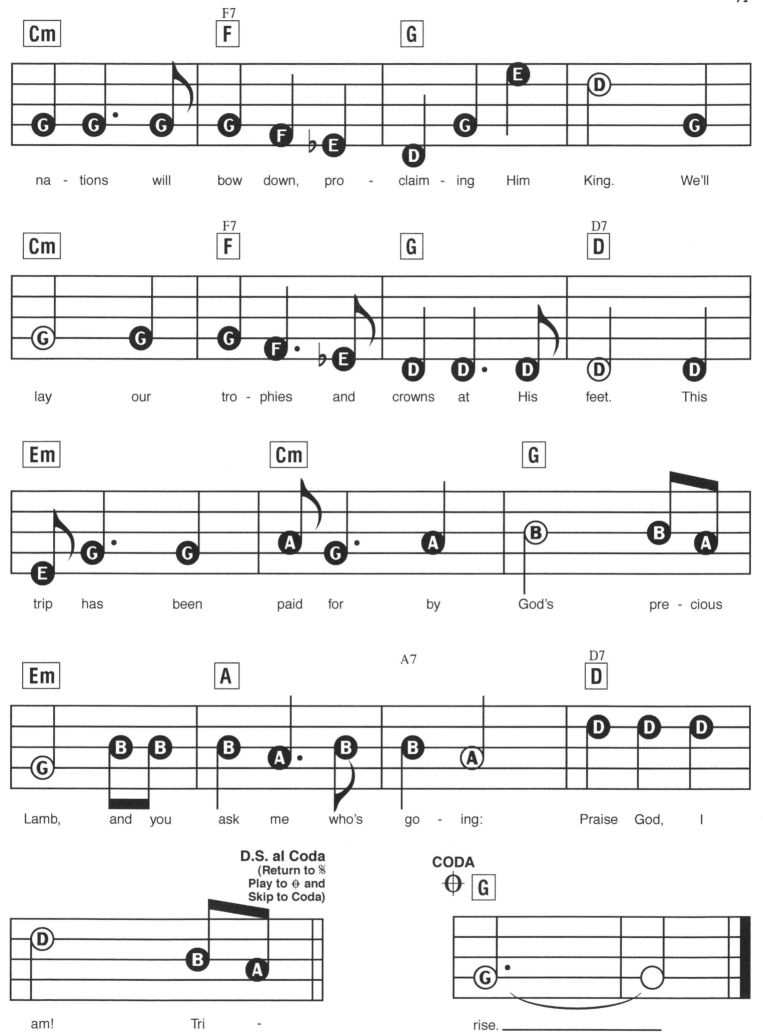

Thank God for the Promise of Spring

Registration 3
Rhythm: Waltz

Words by William J. and Gloria Gaither
Music by William J. Gaither

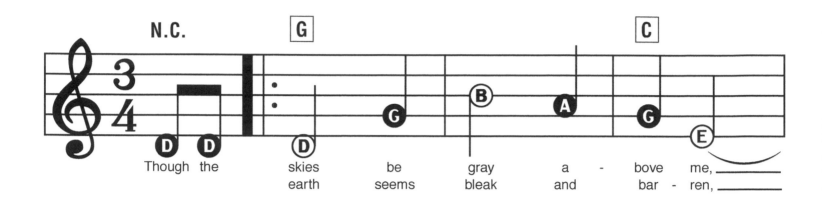

Though the skies be gray a - bove me,
earth be seems bleak and bar - ren,

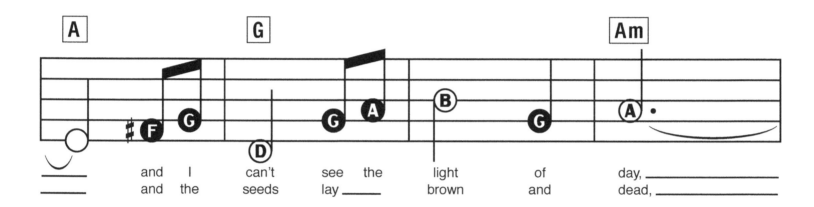

and I can't see the light of day,
and the seeds lay brown and dead,

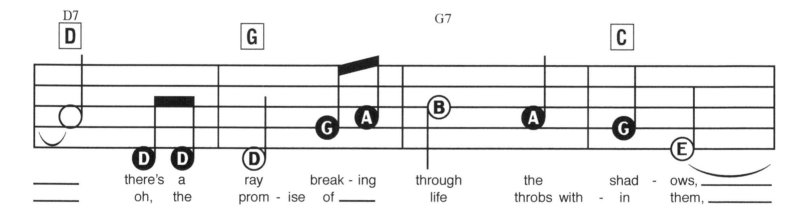

there's a ray break - ing through the shad - ows,
oh, the prom - ise of life throbs with - in them,

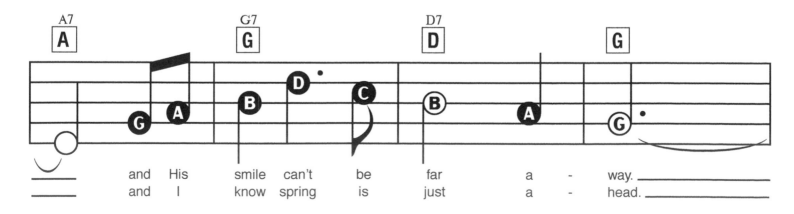

and His smile can't be far a - way.
and I know spring is just a - head.

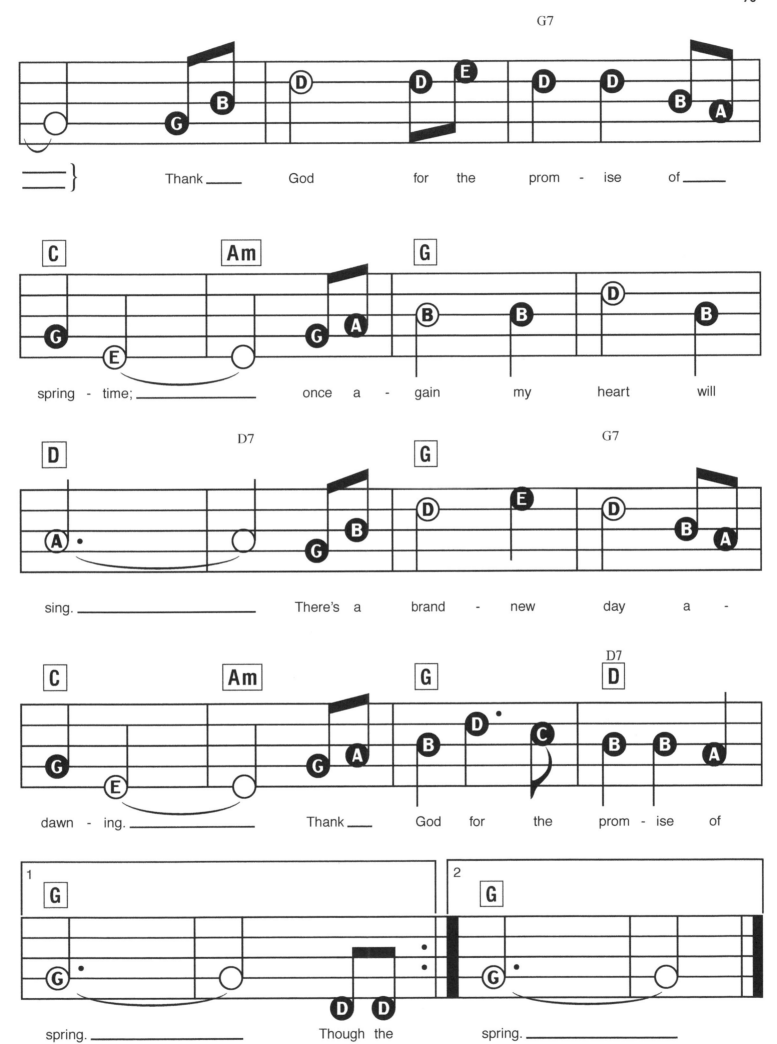

There Will Be Peace in the Valley for Me

Registration 2
Rhythm: Waltz

Words and Music by
Thomas A. Dorsey

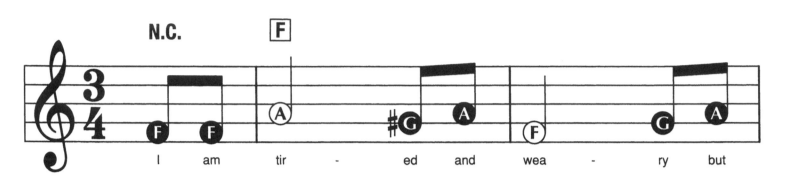

I am tir - ed and wea - ry but

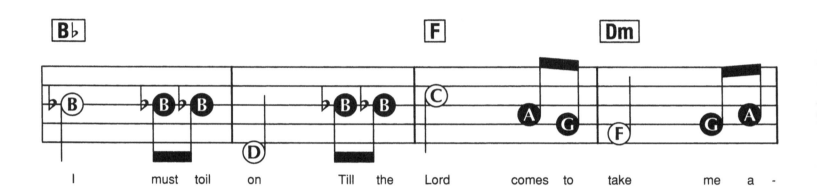

I must toil on Till the Lord comes to take me a -

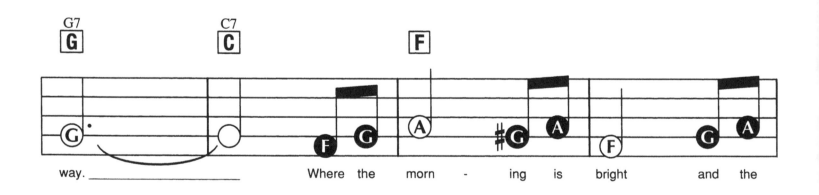

way. _____ Where the morn - ing is bright and the

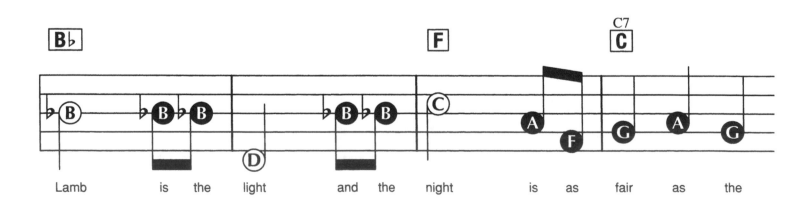

Lamb is the light and the night is as fair as the

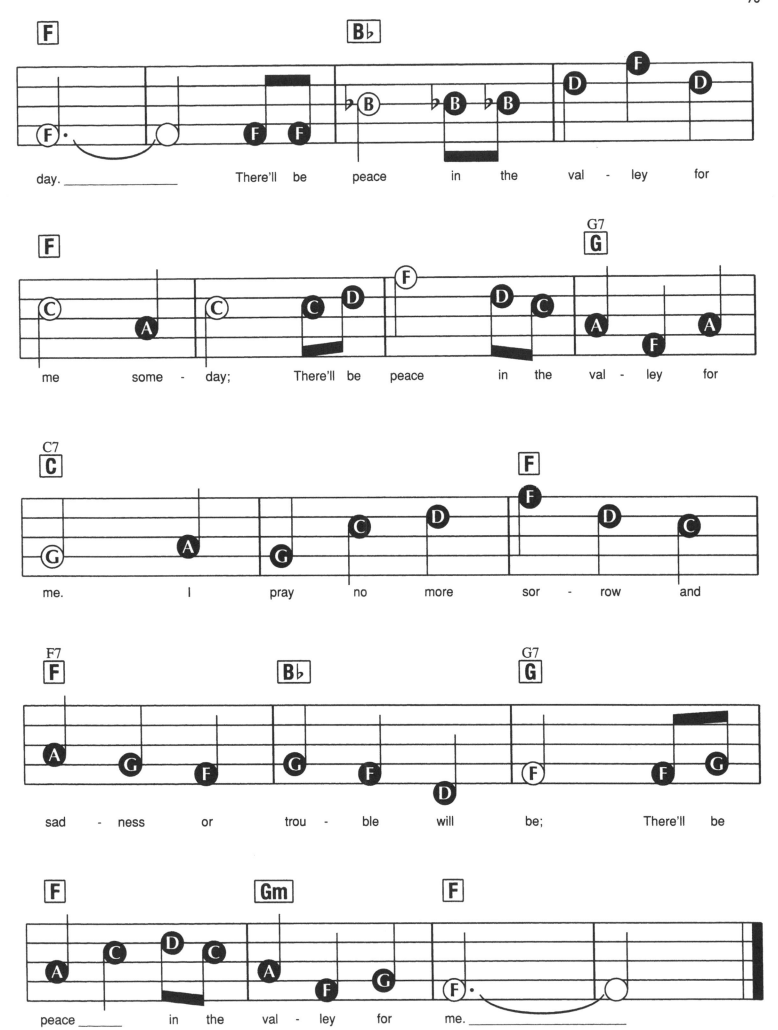

There's Something About That Name

Registration 1
Rhythm: Waltz

Words by William J. and Gloria Gaither
Music by William J. Gaither

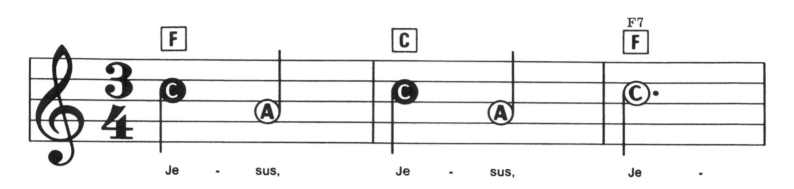

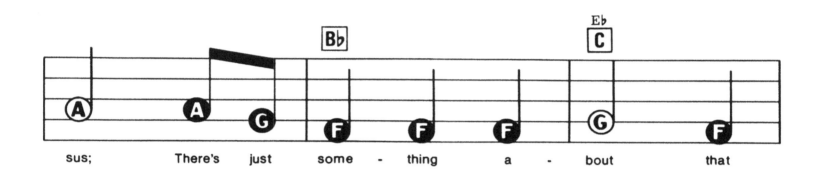

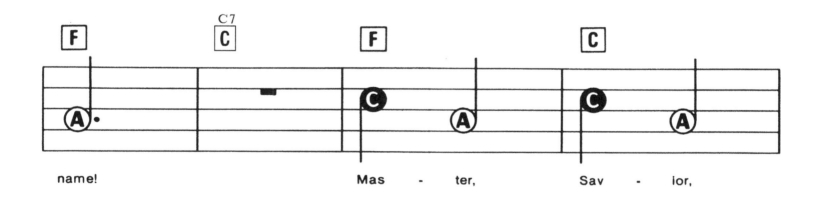

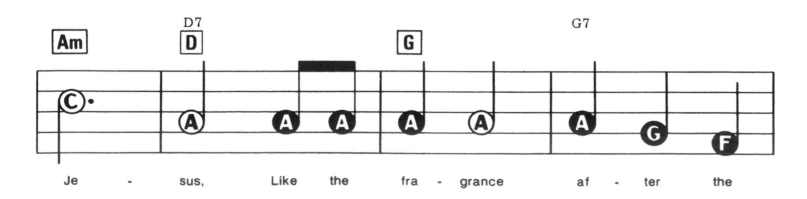

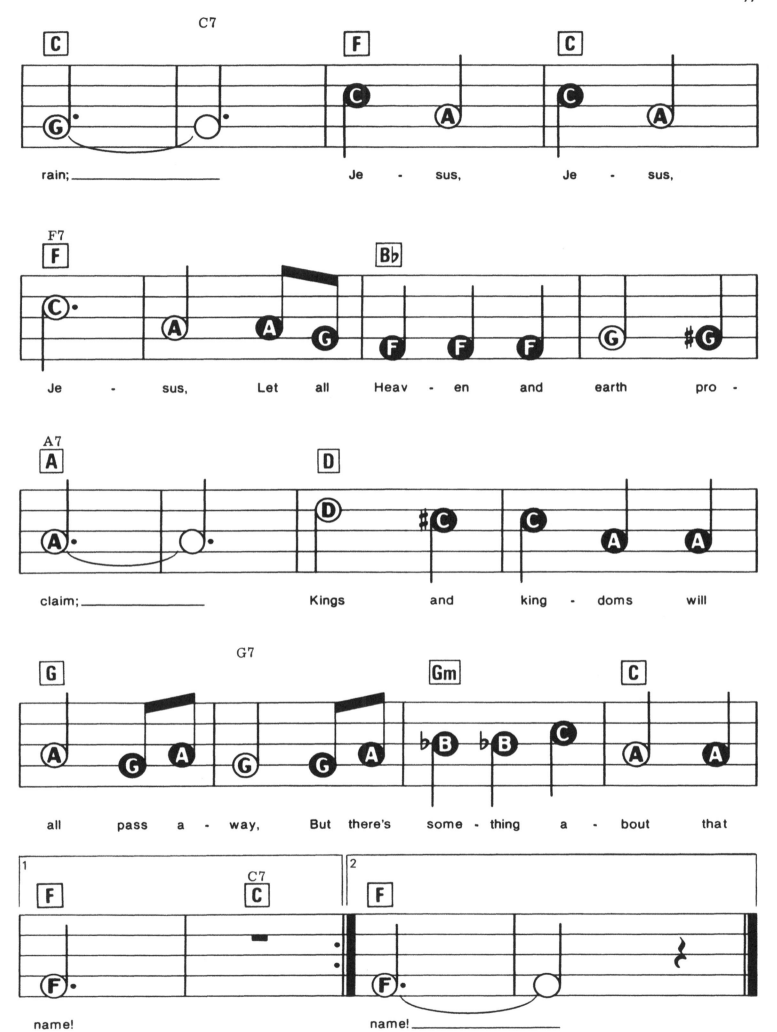

Turn Your Radio On

Registration 4
Rhythm: Fox Trot or Country

Words and Music by
Albert E. Brumley

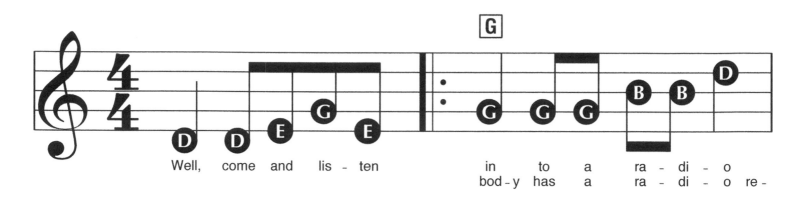

Well, come and lis - ten in to a ra - di - o
bod - y has a ra - di - o re -

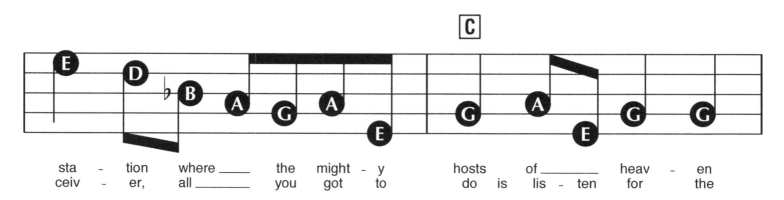

sta - tion where ___ the might - y hosts of ___ heav - en
ceiv - er, all ___ you got to do is lis - ten for the

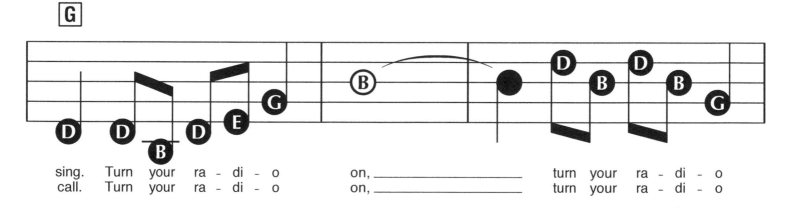

sing. Turn your ra - di - o on, ___ turn your ra - di - o
call. Turn your ra - di - o on, ___ turn your ra - di - o

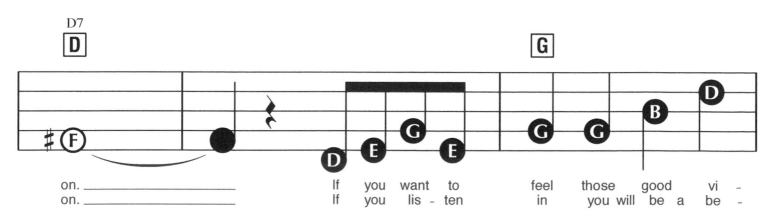

on. ___ If you want to feel those good vi -
on. ___ If you lis - ten in you will be a be -

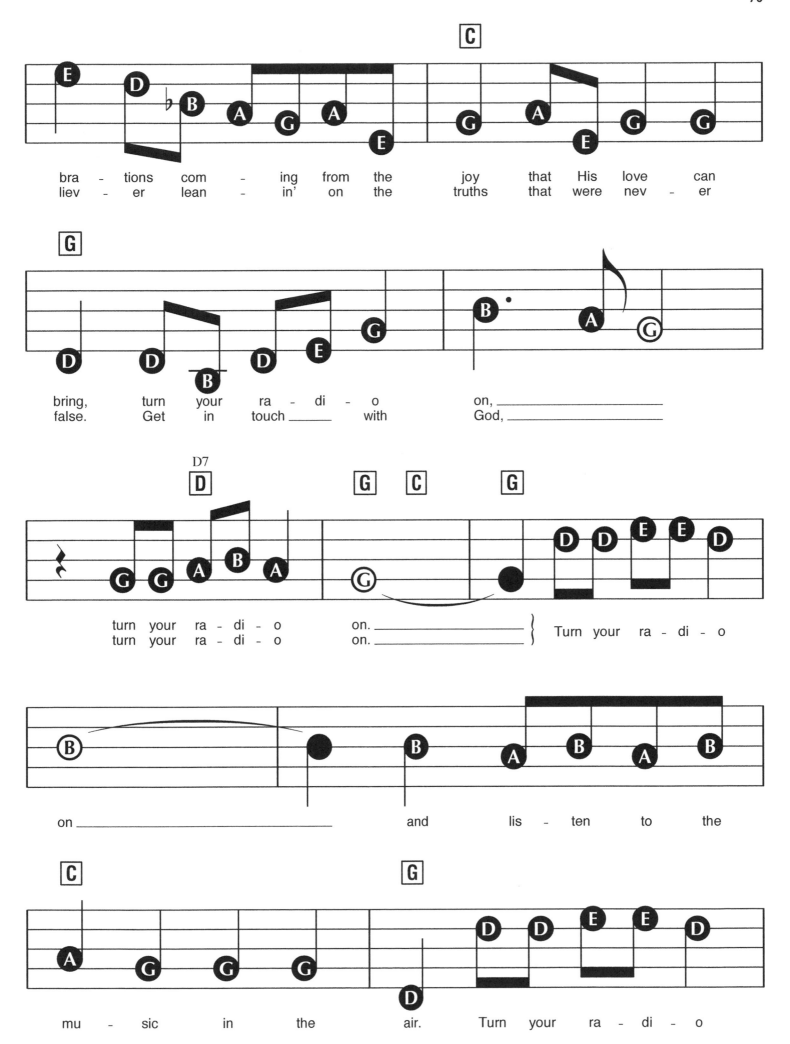

80

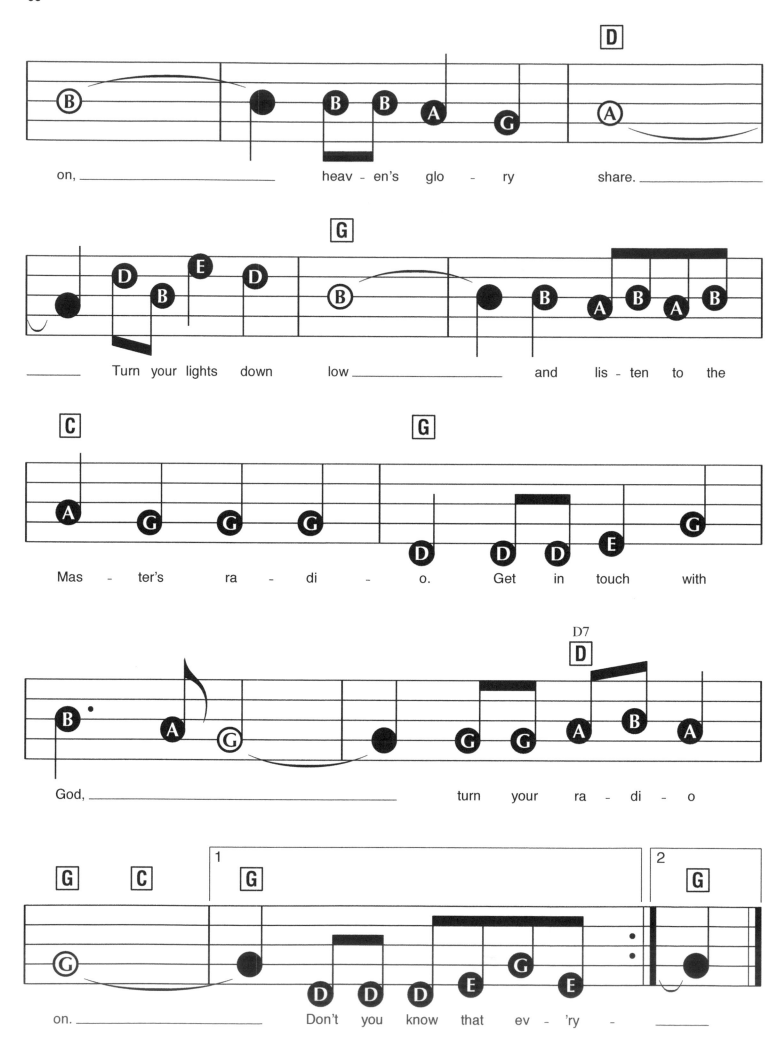

Victory in Jesus

Registration 4
Rhythm: Gospel or Country

Words and Music by
E.M. Bartlett

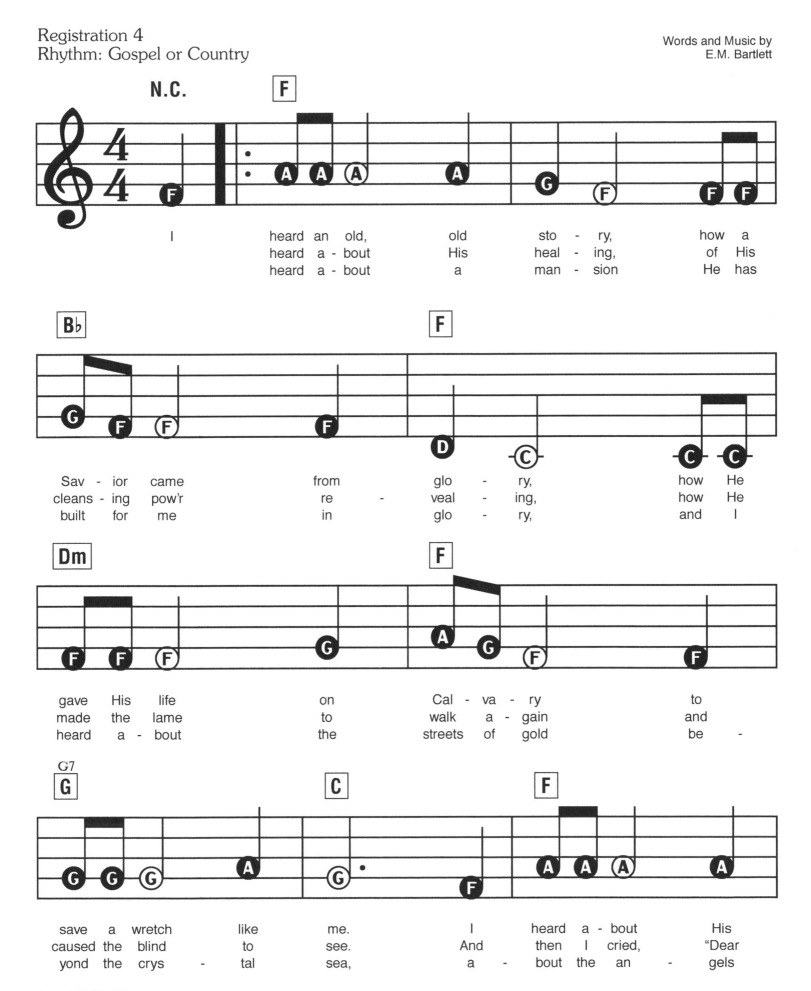

82

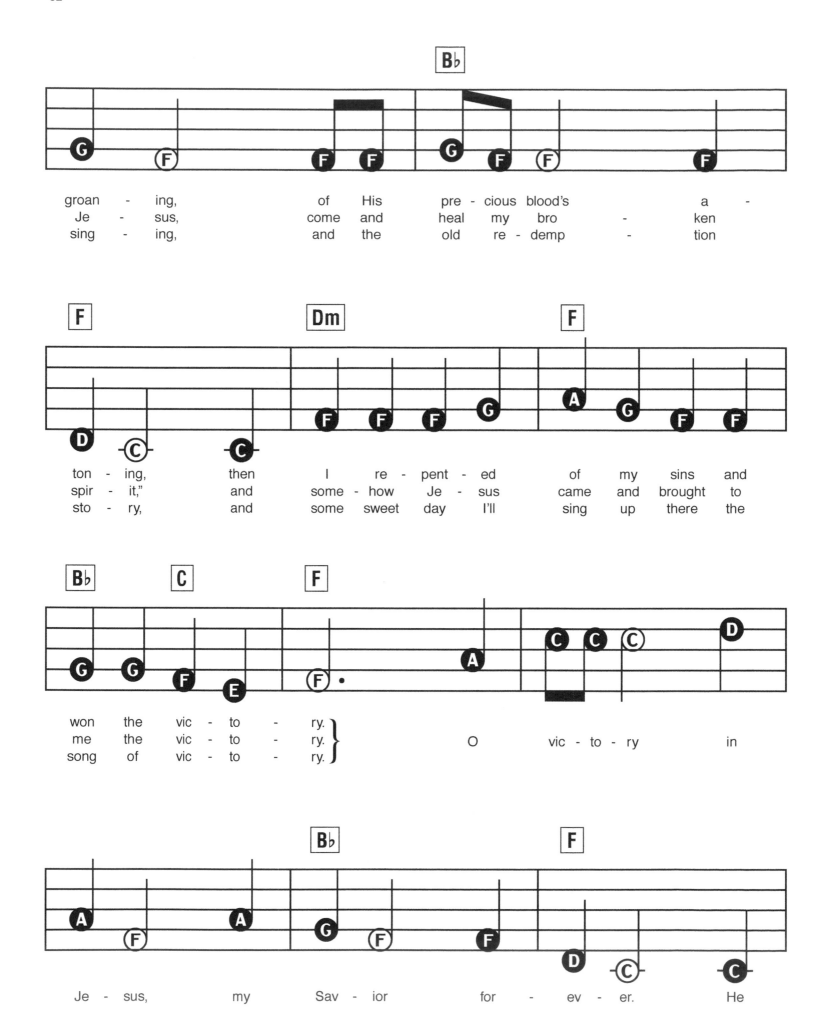

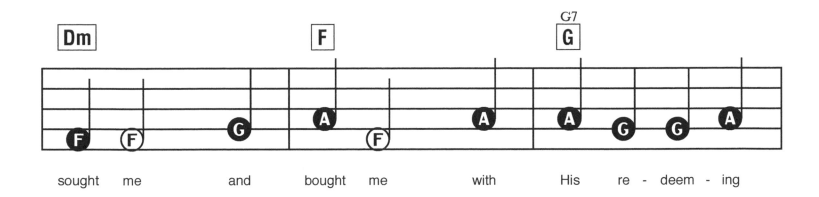

sought me and bought me with His re - deem - ing

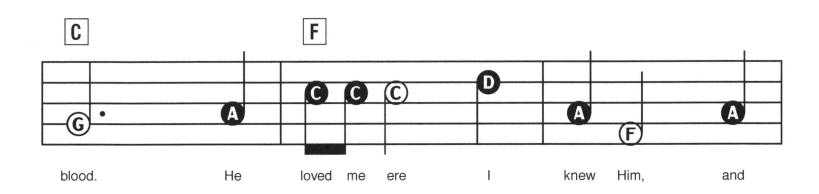

blood. He loved me ere I knew Him, and

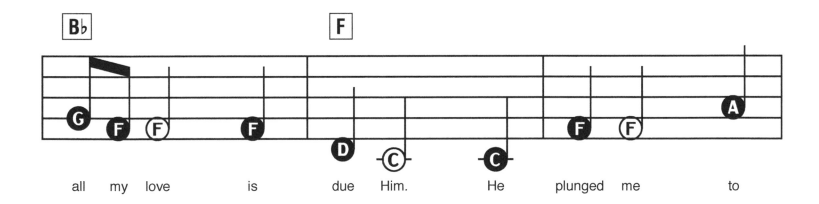

all my love is due Him. He plunged me to

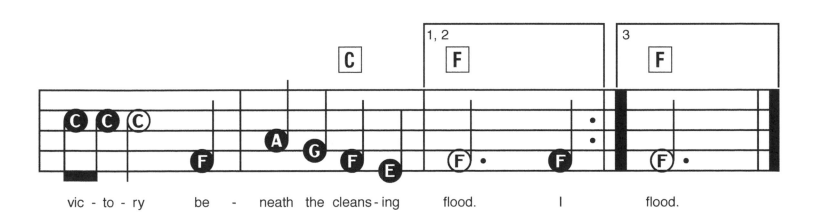

vic - to - ry be - neath the cleans - ing flood. I flood.

The Way That He Loves

Registration 8
Rhythm: Waltz or None

Words and Music by
Elmo W. Mercer

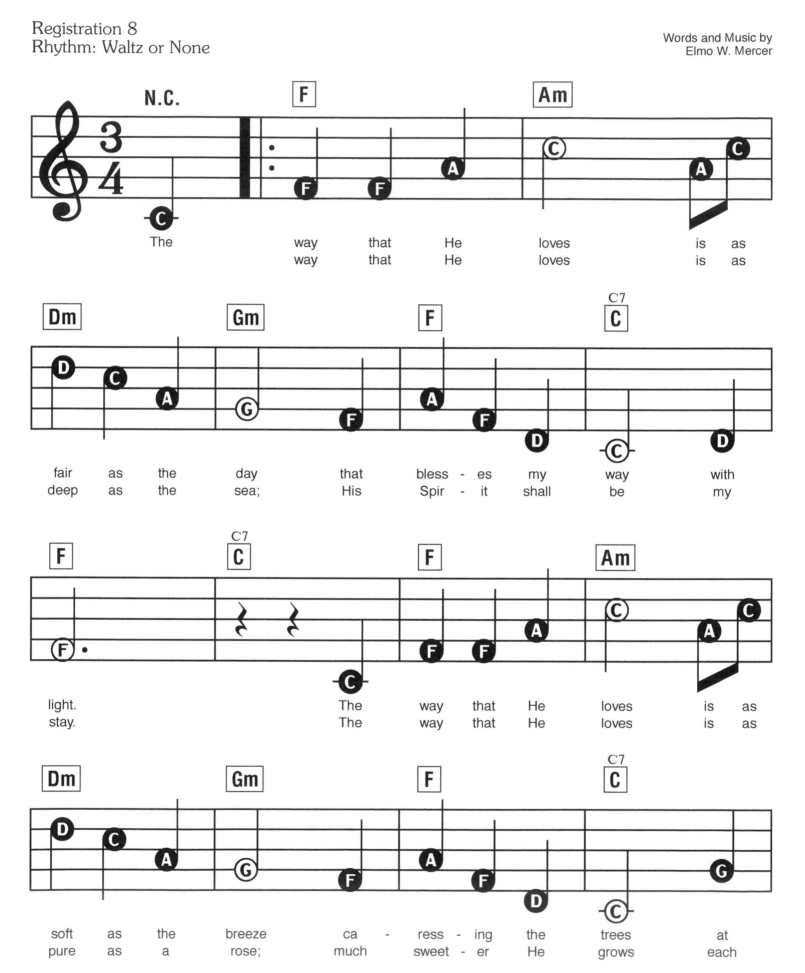

We Are So Blessed

Registration 3
Rhythm: Waltz

Words and Music by Greg Nelson,
Gloria and William J. Gaither

We Have Come Into His House

Registration 1
Rhythm: Slow Rock or Shuffle

Words and Music by
Bruce Ballinger

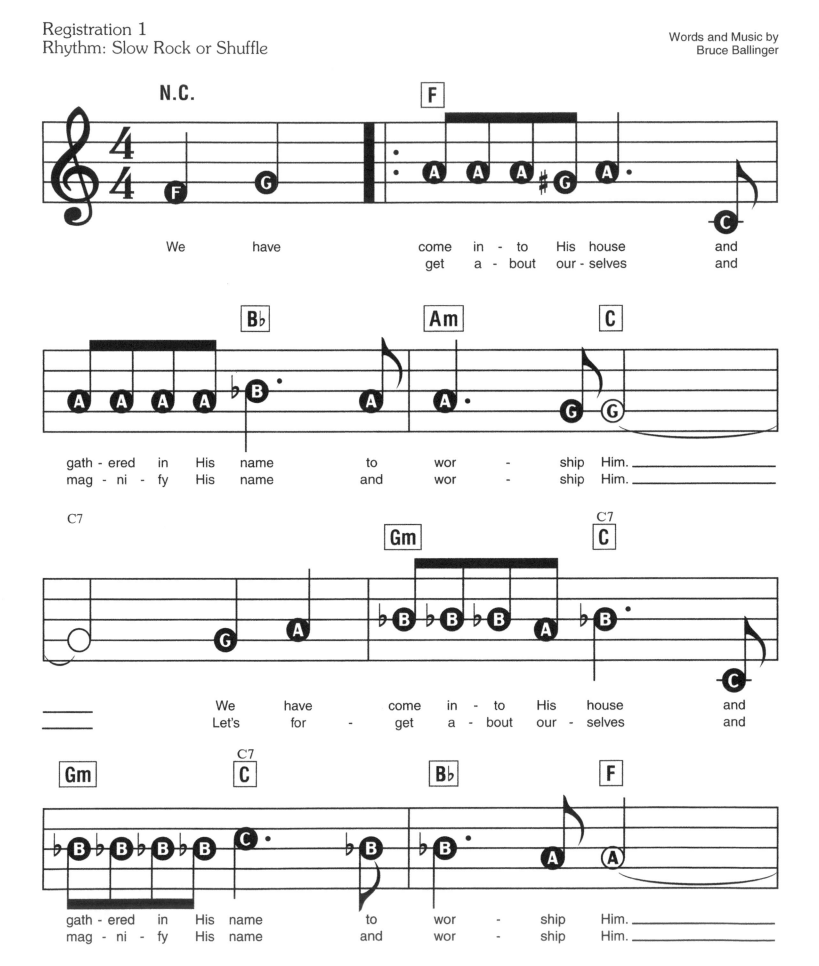

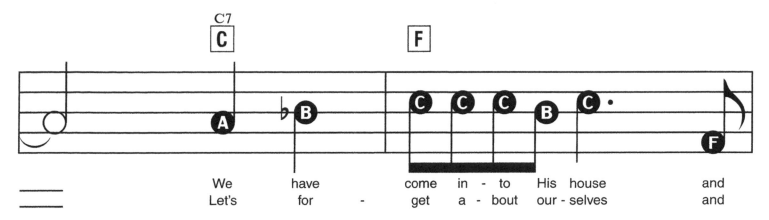

We have come in - to His house and
Let's for - get a - bout our - selves and

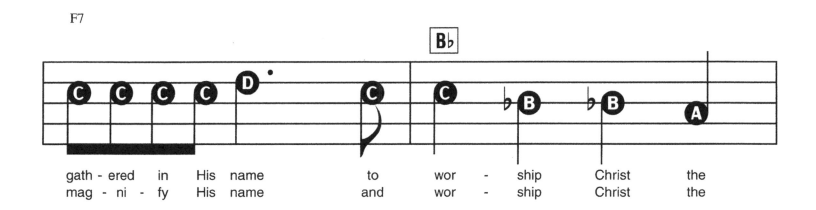

gath - ered in His name to wor - ship Christ the
mag - ni - fy His name and wor - ship Christ Christ the

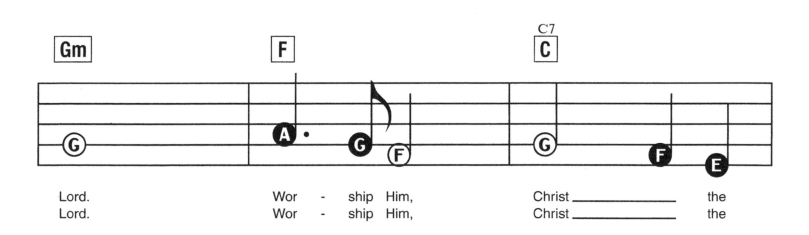

Lord. Wor - ship Him, Christ _____ the
Lord. Wor - ship Him, Christ _____ the

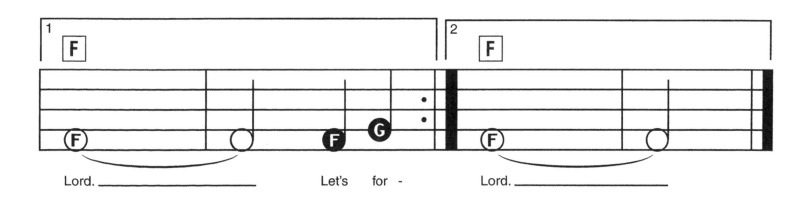

Lord. _____ Let's for -
Lord. _____

What a Day That Will Be

Registration 6
Rhythm: Waltz or None

Words and Music by
Jim Hill

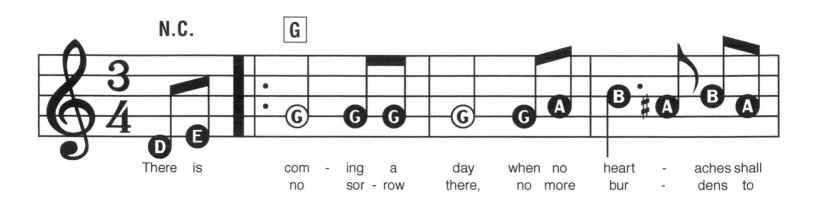

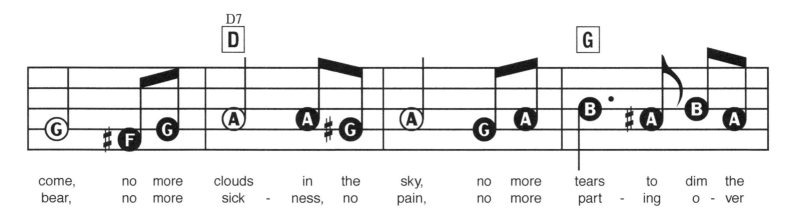

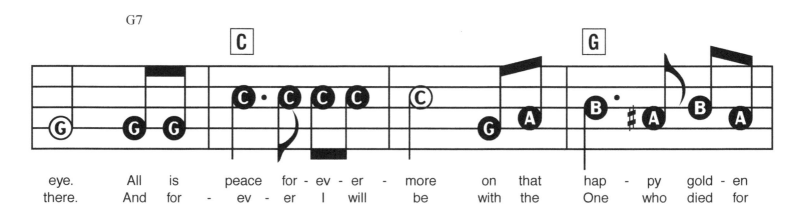

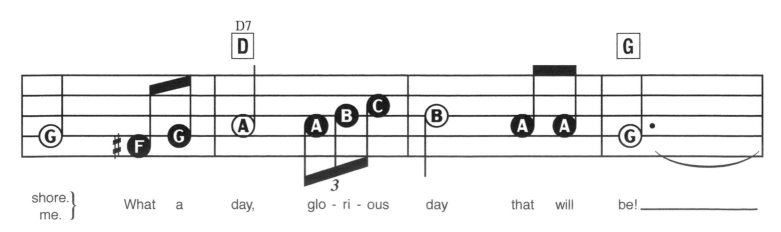

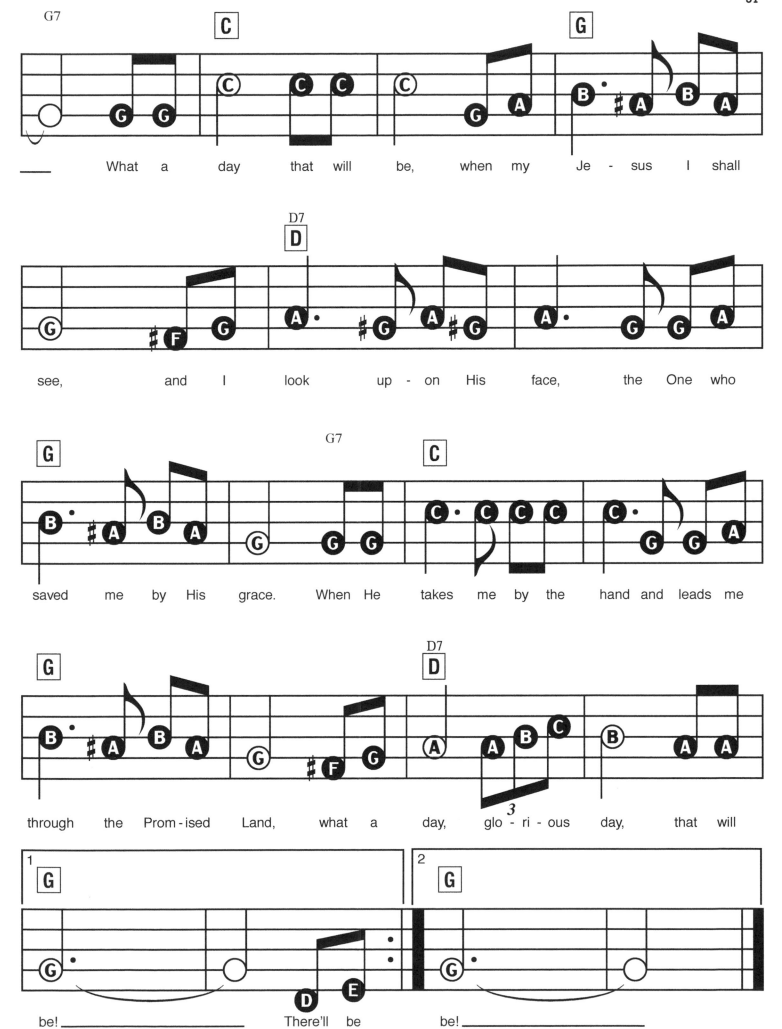

Registration Guide

• Match the Registration number on the song to the corresponding numbered category below. Select and activate an instrumental sound available on your instrument.

• Choose an automatic rhythm appropriate to the mood and style of the song. (Consult your Owner's Guide for proper operation of automatic rhythm features.)

• Adjust the tempo and volume controls to comfortable settings.

Registration

1	Mellow	Flutes, Clarinet, Oboe, Flugel Horn, Trombone, French Horn, Organ Flutes
2	Ensemble	Brass Section, Sax Section, Wind Ensemble, Full Organ, Theater Organ
3	Strings	Violin, Viola, Cello, Fiddle, String Ensemble, Pizzicato, Organ Strings
4	Guitars	Acoustic/Electric Guitars, Banjo, Mandolin, Dulcimer, Ukulele, Hawaiian Guitar
5	Mallets	Vibraphone, Marimba, Xylophone, Steel Drums, Bells, Celesta, Chimes
6	Liturgical	Pipe Organ, Hand Bells, Vocal Ensemble, Choir, Organ Flutes
7	Bright	Saxophones, Trumpet, Mute Trumpet, Synth Leads, Jazz/Gospel Organs
8	Piano	Piano, Electric Piano, Honky Tonk Piano, Harpsichord, Clavi
9	Novelty	Melodic Percussion, Wah Trumpet, Synth, Whistle, Kazoo, Perc. Organ
10	Bellows	Accordion, French Accordion, Mussette, Harmonica, Pump Organ, Bagpipes

FOR ORGANS, PIANOS & ELECTRONIC KEYBOARDS

E-Z PLAY® TODAY

E-Z PLAY® TODAY PUBLICATIONS

*The E-Z Play® Today songbook series is the shortest distance between beginning music and playing fun! Check out this list of highlights and visit **halleonard.com** for a complete listing of all volumes and songlists.*

00102278 1. Favorite Songs with 3 Chords $9.99
00100374 2. Country Sound $12.99
00284446 3. Contemporary Disney $16.99
00100382 4. Dance Band Greats $7.95
00100305 5. All-Time Standards $10.99
00282553 6. Songs of the Beatles $14.99
00100442 7. Hits from Musicals $8.99
00100490 8. Patriotic Songs $8.99
00236235 9. Christmas Time $9.99
00198012 10. Songs of Hawaii $12.99
00137580 11. 75 Light Classical Songs $19.99
00110284 12. Star Wars $10.99
00100248 13. 3-Chord Country Songs $14.99
00100248 14. All-Time Requests $8.99
00241118 15. Simple Songs $14.99
00266435 16. Broadway's Best $12.99
00100415 17. Fireside Singalong $14.99
00149113 18. 30 Classical Masterworks $8.99
00137780 19. Top Country Songs $12.99
00102277 20. Hymns $9.99
00197200 21. Good Ol' Gospel $12.99
00100570 22. Sacred Sounds $8.99
00234685 23. First 50 Songs You Should Play on Keyboard $16.99
00249679 24. Songs with 3 Chords $14.99
00140724 25. Happy Birthday to You & Other Great Songs $10.99
14041364 26. Bob Dylan $12.99
00001236 27. 60 of the Easiest to Play Songs with 3 Chords $9.99
00101598 28. 50 Classical Themes $9.99
00100135 29. Love Songs $9.99
00100030 30. Country Connection $12.99
00100010 31. Big Band Favorites $9.99
00249578 32. Songs with 4 Chords $14.99
00160720 33. Ragtime Classics $9.99
00100122 36. Good Ol' Songs $12.99
00100410 37. Favorite Latin Songs $8.99
00156394 38. Best of Adele $10.99
00159567 39. Best Children's Songs Ever $17.99
00119955 40. Coldplay $10.99
00287762 41. Bohemian Rhapsody $14.99
00100123 42. Baby Boomers Songbook $10.99
00102135 44. Best of Willie Nelson $14.99
00100460 45. Love Ballads $8.99
00156236 46. 15 Chart Hits $12.99
00100007 47. Duke Ellington $8.95
00100343 48. Gospel Songs of Johnny Cash $9.99
00236314 49. Beauty and the Beast $12.99
00102114 50. Best of Patsy Cline $9.99
00100208 51. Essential Songs: 1950s $17.99
00100209 52. Essential Songs: 1960s $19.99
00348318 53. 100 Most Beautiful Christmas Songs $22.99
00199268 54. Acoustic Songs $12.99
00100342 55. Johnny Cash $12.99
00137703 56. Jersey Boys $12.99
00100118 57. More of the Best Songs Ever $19.99
00100285 58. Four-Chord Songs $10.99
00100353 59. Christmas Songs $10.99
00100304 60. Songs for All Occasions $16.99
00100409 62. Favorite Hymns $7.99
00278397 63. Classical Music $7.99
00100223 64. Wicked $12.99
00100217 65. Hymns with 3 Chords $8.99
00232258 66. La La Land $12.99
00100268 68. Pirates of the Caribbean $12.99
00100449 69. It's Gospel $9.99
00100432 70. Gospel Greats $8.99
00236744 71. 21 Top Hits $12.99
00100117 72. Canciones Románticas $10.99
00237558 73. Michael Jackson $12.99
00147049 74. Over the Rainbow & 40 More Great Songs $12.99
00100568 75. Sacred Moments $6.95
00100572 76. The Sound of Music $10.99
00238941 77. Andrew Lloyd Webber $12.99
00100530 78. Oklahoma! $6.95
00248709 79. Roadhouse Country $12.99
00100200 80. Essential Paul Anka $8.95
00100262 82. Big Book of Folk Pop Rock $14.99
00100584 83. Swingtime $7.95
00265416 84. Ed Sheeran $14.99
00100221 85. Cowboy Songs $7.95
00265488 86. Leonard Cohen $12.99
00100286 87. 50 Worship Standards $14.99
00100287 88. Glee $9.99
00100577 89. Songs for Children $9.99
00290104 90. Elton John Anthology $16.99
00100034 91. 30 Songs for a Better World $10.99
00100288 92. Michael Bublé Crazy Love $10.99
00100036 93. Country Hits $12.99
00100219 95. Phantom of the Opera $12.99
00100263 96. Mamma Mia $10.99
00102317 97. Elvis Presley $14.99
00109768 98. Flower Power $16.99
00275360 99. The Greatest Showman $12.99
00282486 100. The New Standards $19.99
00100000 101. Annie $10.99
00286388 102. Dear Evan Hansen $12.99
00119237 103. Two-Chord Songs $9.99
00147057 104. Hallelujah & 40 More Great Songs $14.99
00287417 105. River Flows in You & Other Beautiful Songs $12.99
00139940 106. 20 Top Hits $14.99
00100256 107. The Best Praise & Worship Songs Ever $16.99
00100363 108. Classical Themes $7.99
00102232 109. Motown's Greatest Hits $12.95
00101566 110. Neil Diamond Collection $15.99
00100119 111. Season's Greetings $15.99
00101498 112. Best of the Beatles $21.99
00100134 113. Country Gospel USA $14.99
00100264 114. Pride and Prejudice $9.99
00101612 115. The Greatest Waltzes $9.99
00287931 116. A Star Is Born, La La Land, Greatest Showman & More $14.99
00289026 117. Tony Bennett $14.99
00100136 118. 100 Kids' Songs $14.99
00139985 119. Blues $12.99
00100433 120. Bill & Gloria Gaither $14.95
00100333 121. Boogies, Blues & Rags $9.99
00100146 122. Songs for Praise & Worship $9.99
00100266 123. Pop Piano Hits $14.99
00101440 124. The Best of Alabama $7.95
00100001 125. The Great Big Book of Children's Songs $14.99
00101563 127. John Denver $12.99
00116947 128. John Williams $12.99
00140764 129. Campfire Songs $12.99
00116956 130. Taylor Swift Hits $10.99
00102318 131. Doo-Wop Songbook $12.99
00100258 132. Frank Sinatra: Christmas Collection $10.99
00100306 133. Carole King $12.99
00100226 134. AFI's Top 100 Movie Songs $24.95
00289978 135. Mary Poppins Returns $10.99
00291475 136. Disney Fun Songs $14.99
00100144 137. Children's Movie Hits $9.99
00100038 138. Nostalgia Collection $16.99
00100289 139. Crooners $19.99
00101956 140. Best of George Strait $16.99
00294969 141. A Sentimental Christmas $12.99
00300288 142. Aladdin $10.99
00101946 143. Songs of Paul McCartney $8.99
00140768 144. Halloween $10.99
00100291 145. Traditional Gospel $9.99
00319452 146. The Lion King (2019) $10.99
00147061 147. Great Instrumentals $9.99
00100222 148. Italian Songs $9.99
00329569 149. Frozen 2 $10.99
00100152 151. Beach Boys Greatest Hits $14.99
00101592 152. Fiddler on the Roof $9.99
00140981 153. 50 Great Songs $14.99
00100228 154. Walk the Line $8.95
00101549 155. Best of Billy Joel $12.99
00101769 158. Very Best of John Lennon $12.99
00326434 159. Cats $10.99
00100315 160. Grammy Awards Record of the Year 1958-2011 $19.99
00100293 161. Henry Mancini $10.99
00100049 162. Lounge Music $10.95
00100295 163. Very Best of the Rat Pack $12.99
00277916 164. Best Christmas Songbook $9.99
00101895 165. Rodgers & Hammerstein Songbook $10.99
00149300 166. The Best of Beethoven $8.99
00149736 167. The Best of Bach $8.99
00100148 169. Charlie Brown Christmas $10.99
00100900 170. Kenny Rogers $12.99
00101537 171. Best of Elton John $9.99
00101796 172. The Music Man $9.99
00100321 173. Adele: 21 $12.99
00100229 175. Party Songs $14.99
00100149 176. Charlie Brown Collection $9.99
00100019 177. I'll Be Seeing You $15.99
00102325 179. Love Songs of the Beatles $14.99
00149881 180. The Best of Mozart $8.99
00101610 181. Great American Country Songbook $16.99
00001246 182. Amazing Grace $12.99
00450133 183. West Side Story $9.99
00290252 184. Merle Haggard $14.99
00100151 185. Carpenters $12.99
00101606 186. 40 Pop & Rock Song Classics $14.99
00100155 187. Ultimate Christmas $18.99
00102276 189. Irish Favorites $9.99
00100053 191. Jazz Love Songs $9.99
00123123 193. Bruno Mars $11.99
00124609 195. Opera Favorites $8.99
00101609 196. Best of George Gershwin $14.99
00119857 199. Jumbo Songbook $24.99
00295070 200. Best Songs Ever $19.99
00101540 202. Best Country Songs Ever $17.99
00101541 203. Best Broadway Songs Ever $19.99
00101542 204. Best Easy Listening Songs Ever $17.99
00284127 205. Best Love Songs Ever $17.99
00101570 209. Disney Christmas Favorites $9.99
00100059 210. '60s Pop Rock Hits $14.99
14041777 211. Big Book of Nursery Rhymes & Children's Songs $15.99
00126895 212. Frozen $9.99
00101546 213. Disney Classics $15.99
00101533 215. Best Christmas Songs Ever $22.99
00131100 216. Frank Sinatra Centennial Songbook $19.99
00100040 217. Movie Ballads $9.99
00100156 219. Christmas Songs with Three Chords $9.99
00102190 221. Carly Simon Greatest Hits $8.95
00102080 225. Lawrence Welk Songbook $10.99
00283385 234. Disney Love Songs $12.99
00101581 235. Elvis Presley Anthology $16.99
00100165 236. God Bless America & Other Songs for a Better Nation $26.99
00290209 242. Les Misérables $10.95
00100158 243. Oldies! Oldies! Oldies! $12.99
00100041 245. Simon & Garfunkel $10.99
00100267 246. Andrew Lloyd Webber Favorites $10.99
00100296 248. Love Songs of Elton John $12.99
00102113 251. Phantom of the Opera $14.99
00100203 256. Very Best of Lionel Richie $10.99
00100302 258. Four-Chord Worship $9.99
00286504 260. Mister Rogers' Songbook $9.99
00100235 263. Grand Irish Songbook $19.95
00100063 266. Latin Hits $7.95
00100062 269. Love That Latin Beat $8.99
00101425 272. ABBA Gold Greatest Hits $9.99
00100024 274. 150 of the Most Beautiful Songs Ever $22.99
00102248 275. Classical Hits $8.99
00100186 277. Stevie Wonder $10.99
00100227 278. 150 More of the Most Beautiful Songs Ever $24.99
00100236 279. Alan Jackson $20.99
00100237 280. Dolly Parton $10.99
00100238 281. Neil Young $12.99
00100239 282. Great American Songbook $19.95
00100068 283. Best Jazz Standards Ever $15.95
00281046 284. Great American Songbook: The Singers $19.99
00100271 286. CMT's 100 Greatest Love Songs $24.99
00100244 287. Josh Groban $14.99
00102124 293. Movie Classics $10.99
00100303 295. Best of Michael Bublé $14.99
00100075 296. Best of Cole Porter $9.99
00102130 298. Beautiful Love Songs $9.99
00100077 299. The Vaudeville Songbook $7.99
00259570 301. Kids' Songfest $12.99
00110416 302. More Kids' Songfest $12.99
00100275 305. Rod Stewart $12.99
00102147 306. Irving Berlin Collection $16.99
00100276 307. Gospel Songs with 3 Chords $8.99
00100194 309. 3-Chord Rock 'n' Roll $9.99
02501515 312. Barbra Streisand $10.99
00100197 315. VH1's 100 Greatest Songs of Rock & Roll $19.95
00100234 316. E-Z Play® Today White Pages $27.99
00100277 325. Taylor Swift $10.99
00100249 328. French Songs $8.95
00100251 329. Antonio Carlos Jobim $7.99
00102275 330. The Nutcracker Suite $8.99
00100092 333. Great Gospel Favorites $8.99
00100273 336. Beautiful Ballads $19.99
00100278 338. The Best Hymns Ever $19.99
00100084 339. Grease Is Still the Word $12.99
00100235 346. The Big Book of Christmas Songs $16.99
00100089 349. The Giant Book of Christmas Songs $9.95
00100087 354. The Mighty Big Book of Christmas Songs $12.95
00100088 355. Smoky Mountain Gospel Favorites $9.99
00100093 358. Gospel Songs of Hank Williams $7.95
00100095 359. 100 Years of Song $19.99
00100096 360. More 100 Years of Song $19.95
00159568 362. Songs of the 1920s $19.99
00159569 363. Songs of the 1930s $19.99
00159570 364. Songs of the 1940s $19.99
00159571 365. Songs of the 1950s $19.99
00159572 366. Songs of the 1960s $19.99
00159573 367. Songs of the 1970s $19.99
00159574 368. Songs of the 1980s $19.99
00159575 369. Songs of the 1990s $19.99
00159576 370. Songs of the 2000s $19.99
00339094 370. Songs of the 2010s $19.99
00100103 375. Songs of Bacharach & David $9.99
00100107 392. Disney Favorites $19.99
00100108 393. Italian Favorites $9.99
00100111 394. Best Gospel Songs Ever $19.99
00100115 400. Classical Masterpieces $11.99

HAL•LEONARD®

Prices, contents and availability subject to change without notice

0421
330